ABUNDANT AND FREE

Seeing Life Through
the Lens of Grace

Scott Prickett

Abundant and Free
by Scott Prickett
Copyright ©2017
All rights reserved by M. Scott Prickett
Visit www.scottprickett.com

All Scripture quotations, unless otherwise indicated, are taken from the Holy Bible, New International Version®, NIV®. Copyright ©1973, 1978, 1984, 2011 by Biblica, Inc.™ Used by permission of Zondervan. All rights reserved worldwide. www.zondervan.com.

Scripture quotations marked "ESV" are from The ESV® Bible (The Holy Bible, English Standard Version®), copyright © 2001 by Crossway, a publishing ministry of Good News Publishers. Used by permission. All rights reserved."

No part of this book may be reproduced or transmitted in any form or by any means, graphic, electronic, or mechanical, including photocopying, recording, taping or by any information storage retrieval system without the permission, in writing, from the author.

Printed in the United States of America.

TABLE OF CONTENTS

1	Life From Death	9
2	The Flow of Grace	17
3	The Joy of Winning	25
4	Our New Reality	33
5	Restraining Our Depravity	43
6	Persevering Through Trials	53
7	Understanding Things	63
8	Doing Great and Glorious Things	71
9	Abundant and Free	81
10	The Lens of Grace	91
11	Love You Some You	99
12	The Pain of Appropriation	107
13	The Transfer of Grace	117
14	The Common Ground of Grace	125
15	Spotting the Issue	133
16	Greater Glory	143

INTRODUCTION

The evidence against us is compelling. For some more adept at walking the straight and narrow, this conclusion is the result of a close examination of our thoughts and motives; for others of us, a passing glance is all that's needed. All of us—no matter who you are, how you were raised or how pure your intentions—have acted contrary to the purpose of our design and stumbled or willingly jumped outside the boundaries prescribed for living. How you got there or how far off the path you move makes no difference. If we were burdened with keeping the Law, we could all be dragged into the public square for prosecution.

In the book of John[1] we read about such "public square prosecution" when the Pharisees bring a woman caught in the act of adultery to Jesus as He was teaching in the Temple courts. There was compelling, however awkward, evidence of her guilt. She was guilty, she knew it, and everyone present knew it. Her accusers brought her to Jesus to see if He would defend her. It was a losing case for Him, they assumed, as the Law was clear and the evidence abundant.

When practicing law, I routinely defended people who had broken the law. In those days, people—mostly Christian people—often asked how I could morally support my decision to be an advocate for the immoral. The answer was easy. Jesus is our advocate, even though we did "it" in some form or fashion. The case is airtight against us, but He doesn't turn from us. The chance to be an advocate for guilty people was the chance to stand beside them, just as Jesus stands beside us.

In the case of the woman caught in adultery, Jesus' method of defense was peculiar. As her accusers loudly proclaimed the woman's guilt, Jesus silently stooped down and wrote in the dirt with His finger. The Pharisees would not relent; they continued to batter Jesus with the question of what they should do to the woman in light of the Law. After a short time, Jesus stood and invited anyone without sin to begin the prescribed punishment of stoning by throwing the first rock. Then, He stooped down and continued writing in the dirt.

No one could throw the first stone. One by one, the crowd dispersed until only Jesus and the woman remained. Interestingly, verse 9 of John 8 says it was the older men who left first. The older men left first because they had sinned the most, if for no other reason than they had lived the longest so they had the most practice.

Writing in the dirt was the primary tactic Jesus used in defense of the woman. As odd as it seems, Jesus' act of using His finger to write on the earth was a foreshadowing of the exchange He was here to make.

God had written in the earth with His finger previously, and here He was doing it again.

The first time God's finger wrote on the earth was when He wrote the Ten Commandments on stone tablets, some of the very writings the Pharisees hoped to use to condemn the woman. God wrote the Law twice, as Moses broke the first set of tablets. Now, here He is, in the form of Jesus, again writing in the earth, again twice. What He wrote was "grace upon grace" (John 1:16), just as He had written the Law, and then wrote it again. Perfect satisfaction; it is finished.

The first time God wrote in the earth, He wrote the Law; the second time, He wrote grace. Jesus came to satisfy the Law for us, since we can't just as the old men of John 8:9 couldn't. Our perspectives of God and people (starting with ourselves) are evident in what we "write" with our words and attitudes. We are either writing law or grace, and we can only write what we first receive. Realizing that we are not unlike the woman Jesus refused to condemn allows us to receive grace just as it allowed me to defend those who did "it," too.

Chapter 1
LIFE FROM DEATH

I had prayed "the prayer" hundreds of times since I first asked Jesus to save and change me when I was eight years old. I'd even been baptized as proof of my sincerity. And I was sincere: I sincerely wanted to go to heaven and avoid "an eternity of hell." What eight-year-old doesn't? For that matter, what person of any age doesn't?

As I grew, my efforts toward religion led predictably to a life of guilt and shame, not transformation. I was empty inside. I knew something wasn't right in my heart because I was never at peace. So I tried harder. I determined over and over again I'd "do better," but couldn't shake my patterns of behavior. Every failure brought more guilt and shame until frustration from the effort hardened my heart to hope.

The result in my early adult life was a soul of selfishness and purposelessness, bearing the only possible fruits of anger, bitterness and self-protection. I retreated to shelter through alcohol and protected myself with a harsh tone and offensive posture to keep anyone from coming too close. My life was a cycle of living (if you could call it that) from one party to the next where all that mattered was how much "fun" I could have.

The parties and "fun" helped me avoid having to consider what I had become and was becoming. I was out of control, stumbling down a path that alternated between hangovers and the next weekend's party. I was miserable and I knew it.

Then in January 2001, my sister called. Our 18-year-old cousin, Bryan, was very sick and in the hospital. Over the next 12 hours of arranging a flight home, reports got worse. The doctors estimated Bryan's chance of recovery at ten percent. By the time my flight took off, he was gone.

The unexpected death at such an early age of someone I loved hit hard. In the days after his funeral, I began to look at my life through a new lens. I began to search for purpose as never before. "Why am I here? Where am I headed? Will my life make any difference to anybody?" I needed answers.

I soon learned Bryan made a public decision to follow Jesus just weeks before he died. The timing of his salvation such a short time before his death, even before he became sick, struck me as nothing short of a miracle. Pondering this miracle, little by little something inside me started to change. After years of indifference and arrogance, I began to have an awareness of purpose greater than my carnal desires.

I Want That!

Life was being born of death. The destructive plans of evil were turning into victory for righteousness. Instead of hurt and anger, selfishness and hopelessness, I was experiencing real forgiveness and healing for the first time in my life.

About this time, I was considering going to a part-time, evening law school offered by a local Christian college. While there one day, I picked up one of their brochures. As I looked through the pamphlet, my eyes landed on Jeremiah 29:11: *"'For I know the plans I have for you,' declares the Lord, 'plans to prosper you and not to harm you, plans to give you hope and a future.'"*

Everything within me all but shouted: "Yes! That's it! I want **that**!"

I almost fell out of my chair when I read those words. I wanted hope, I wanted a future, and here was God's Word telling me that's exactly what He plans for me.

All doubt of the reality of a God who loved me and wanted relationship with me disappeared into nothingness as my spirit heard Him lovingly call to me in those words. Overwhelming gratitude and a greater hunger to know

Him and be known by Him replaced my uncertainty. I was seeking God and He was revealing Himself to me. I was trying to draw near to Him and He was now drawing near to me. He heard the cry of my heart and answered.

I looked up the verse from Jeremiah in the Bible and found "the rest of the story" in verses 12 and 13: *"Then you will call on me and come and pray to me, and I will listen to you. You will seek me and find me when you seek me with all your heart."* I was no Biblical scholar, but I knew "all" of my heart meant "all." No more compromise.

For years, I'd taken exception to the hypocrisy of the church. I used the failure of man and weakness of people to justify my denial of the living God. Now I was pushing all my chips to the middle of the table. I was going all in.

I gave up and died to me. The arrogant, out of control self-protection and self-promotion gave way to the grace of Jesus. As I died to the old man, He breathed the life of the new man into me. I was born again through encountering the grace of Jesus. After all the arrogance and all the parties, Jesus was welcoming me home without judgment, disgrace, shame or condemnation. Tears rolled down my cheeks as I knew what grace was for the first time in my life.

Years earlier, a friend gave me a copy of the New Testament, and I'd dismissively relegated it to a desolate spot on my bookshelf. Somehow, it had survived several moves, always taking its place toward the end of a shelf I never looked at. That Book's time had come. I pulled it out and started a journey that has been the most exhilarating, challenging and rewarding one of my life.

There were times of just me and that Bible when I would get on my knees, earnestly seeking God. His Word is true and He began to meet me as I chased Him. I didn't have to get "right" or sober or clean or anything. I just had to give up. I did.

I became consumed with a hunger to know Him, not just know about Him and not just for the purpose of going to heaven, but also to know Him as my Friend and Father.

- I read how God wants good things for me.
- I read of the purposes He has for me in the context of His Kingdom.
- I read of the relationship with the Father that is available through Jesus.

The more I came to know Him, the more I realized what following Jesus is supposed to look like. It isn't putting on dress pants and a nice shirt on Sunday mornings. It's putting off our old nature so the world can see His glory. It's not about a set of rules to live by. It's about a Savior to live with. It's not a try-fail-repeat pattern until one day we go to heaven. It's a receive-give-repeat adventure that brings heaven to earth.

Casual Kills You

God invites us into the fullness of life. He invites us on an adventure and gives us a treasure map. Piece by piece we see what the clues on the map mean. It's the depth of this adventure and the riches of the treasure that change destinies. The adventure isn't a safe, sterile and happily-ever-after, robot-like faith. It's having the courage to put it all on the altar for a Creator and His creation in need of a Savior.

If you've ever thought Christianity was boring, now is the time to reconsider. Christianity is not a casual Sunday morning outing. Casual kills you from the inside out. The Christian adventure is all or nothing. It's burning your ships of return, grabbing Jesus' hand and stepping off the cliff of predictability.

God's ways are not our ways. Leaving "normal" is scary. On the other hand, exchanging a life of hopelessness on the road of despair for an adventure to unknown heights with the King of Kings is the best deal we'll ever get. That's exactly the deal He's offering.

The grace of Jesus draws us to salvation, and then leads us into the adventure-filled, miraculous life for which we're created and to which we're called. Walking in relationship with Him, we discover the incalculable benefits of His grace. His grace is more than the key to heaven's gates. Jesus invites each of us into the epic adventure of eternity and the only promise is Him. Everything else is up in the air. Interested? If so, tell Him, jump in and hold on.

I pray and believe God will speak to you in the pages of this book. I pray and hope you'll take a single step of faith, no matter where you are or aren't in your relationship with Him. It might be as easy as a prayer telling Him you just don't get it or you're angry with Him or whatever is on your heart. He can handle it and will meet you at the point that you step out in faith, which is different for each of us.

That tiny step is all it takes to start walking with Him on the journey of your life. Listen to the truth and love He is speaking to your heart. Acknowledge, maybe for the first time, that He *is* speaking to your heart. No matter if you're in a jail with bars or the jail of corporate greed and suburban compromise, allow Him to free and save you. Allow Him to redirect you from the path to nowhere you've been walking onto the path of destiny. Just say "Yes" to the call from His Spirit to yours.

I am still walking this out. On the journey, I sometimes think of my young cousin, who left this world much earlier than expected. Bryan's life made a difference. His story is part of my story. His testimony of hope in salvation spoke to me and opened my heart to the same Hope. That testimony of hope and purpose multiplies in others so the legacy grows. By the grace of Jesus, it's a legacy of life triumphing over death.

Nuggets from this Chapter

- Fulfilling religious ceremonies doesn't bring new life.
- The grace of Jesus invites us back into the love of the Father.
- When we are born again, we are born into an entirely new Kingdom.
- Within the Kingdom of God, there is a plan and a purpose for our lives.
- Christianity is an all-or-nothing proposition with life or death in the balance.

Chapter 2

THE FLOW OF GRACE

Currently, I am a pastor and ministry leader. Before working as a minister, I was an officer in the Army, owned my own business and worked as an attorney. Not all at the same time, of course. When I was a criminal defense lawyer, my clients were either court-appointed or self-paying. The state paid me a set fee to represent appointed clients. I was paid on a per case basis by the paying clients.

The amount I made representing one paying client often was more than what I made representing 100 court-appointed clients in a month. Though I made more money working for the paying clients, I loved representing the assigned clients. The chance to stand with someone no one else would stand with and give a voice to the voiceless was rewarding beyond money.

As I mentioned earlier, people often would shake their head in confusion or disapproval and ask something like, "How can a lawyer, especially a Christian lawyer, defend guilty people?" This reaction to my occupation always surprised me. The fact that people don't have an appetite for criminal defense work isn't what shocked me. It's not a profession everyone should pursue. What stunned me then and stuns me now is the fact that those who most often voice this opinion are Christians; people loyal to their faith, who want to be known as loyal to God in their everyday lives.

Their "comparative innocence" allows them to justify their presumed superiority. They take the moral high ground because, from their perspective, they have nothing in common with the criminal whose constitutionally guaranteed legal defense shocks them. This platform of comparison allows them to form an opinion of being "better than."

The reason these statements from this group baffle me is that the very faith they trumpet opposes the superiority they presume and justify. Their faith is based on grace, yet the lens through which they choose to view criminal defendants is based on justice. Without grace, they'd be as guilty as anyone locked in any prison. Their offenses might not bring criminal charges, but they'd be guilty just the same. Only by the grace of Jesus can they hope to overcome the punishment they would otherwise suffer.

Connected to the Invisible

Grace, love and fellowship connect us to an almighty God and to one another. Holy Spirit reveals their connection and interaction in Paul's closing in the book of 2 Corinthians: *"May the grace of the Lord Jesus Christ, and the love of God, and the fellowship of the Holy Spirit be with you all"* (2 Corinthians 13:14).

- **The fellowship of Holy Spirit is here and now.** Fellowship is intimate and sharing. It's interactive and intertwined. It's God with us, living life and ever-present. It's our invitation into the adventure by evidence of His present reality.

- **The grace of Jesus is our way into the purpose of our existence.** It's a benefit we haven't earned. It's the manifestation of love through sacrifice, and we get a reward we could never imagine. It makes the unapproachable inviting.

- **The love of God is His purpose for us.** He's a Dad, and He loves us. His love for us is what everything has always been about. He takes joy in the joy we find in Him. He is good, and He is for us more than we could be on our best day as parents.

The fellowship of Holy Spirit, the grace of Jesus and the love of the Father agree. Holy Spirit draws us in to Jesus, and Jesus restores us to the Father. When we know His love, we can give love. With God as our Source, we love and worship Him while loving others. We are changed by His love and make Him the object of our affection by receiving His affection.

We all want to know God; it's how we're made. We have an inborn "God want" within us. That want gets hijacked for many and they try to bury it but it's always there. That desire engrained in our design is what calls us into adventure beyond the feedback of the visible toward the wonder of the invisible.

The good news is we're now connected to the invisible God we desire through the visible manifestation of Jesus. We no longer must wonder about this once seemingly distant Supreme Being. Through Jesus, we know God's character in the flesh. Jesus explains this in John 14:5–7:

> *"Thomas said to him, 'Lord, we don't know where you are going, so how can we know the way?' Jesus answered, 'I am the way and the truth and the life. No one comes to the Father except through me. If you really know me, you will know my Father as well. From now on, you do know him and have seen him.'"*

Grace Distributors

The Father revealed through Jesus is great news as we attempt to satisfy our "God want." Still, truly knowing Him may seem difficult if all we do is read about the life of Jesus two thousand years ago. We move closer to knowing God through not only through studying the life of Jesus, but we have an opportunity to know God intimately as we experience Him.

God came *to* us as Jesus, and because of Jesus, His Spirit now lives *in* us. God was embodied as a man two thousand years ago. He is alive and visible through us today. If we pay attention to the Spirit of God coming through us and others, we can know Him better and differently.

Just after Jesus answered Thomas in the passage above, He tells Philip in verses 15–20:

> *"If you love me, keep my commands. And I will ask the Father, and he will give you another advocate to help you and be with you forever— the Spirit of truth. The world cannot accept him because it neither sees him nor knows him. But you know him, for he lives with you and will be in you. I will not leave you as orphans; I will come to you. Before long, the world will not see me anymore, but you will see me. Because I live, you also will live. On that day you will realize that I am in my Father, and you are in me, and I am in you"* (John 14:15–20).

God was manifest in human form in Jesus, and Jesus is manifest in human form through us. We are carriers of His Holy Spirit, vessels of His manifestation. We know Jesus better by knowing others, and we share Jesus by sharing ourselves.

The visible comes from the invisible. To realize the invisible we engage with the visible. In other words, to know the fellowship of Holy Spirit, we must be in fellowship with others. The satisfaction of our core desire to know God occurs in interaction with humanity.

Fellowship through authentic connection and relationship requires grace, because others are flawed and so are we. Connecting with them helps us realize the connection we have to Holy Spirit, Who leads us to the grace of Jesus. Grace gives us the chance to live in relationship with Him as well as each other. That same grace connects us to the love of the Father.

We know His love and become distributors of His love in the same way we become distributors of grace: through relationships. It's a cycle of fellowship, grace and love flowing between people in agreement with the Source of grace and love. God supplies us so we can multiply Him. As we multiply Him with others, we know Him more in and for ourselves. The more we operate in His nature, the more we walk in His commandments (John 14:15).

The foundational benefit of grace is Jesus resides with us as we give our life for His, and our connection to Him satisfies the eternal design of our soul. We are distributors of Jesus' grace and the Father's love. We get to go to heaven, but we also get to know the first fruits of heaven here and now as His Spirit empowers and accompanies us. We are ambassadors of heaven to earth for our King and His Kingdom.

Our awareness of purpose and of the benefits of grace isn't achieved in a classroom, not even a Bible study classroom. It's achieved through connection with others. Understanding the benefits of grace, we no longer wonder how an attorney defends a guilty person. Instead we realize the freedom we have when the Advocate stands with us. We no longer avoid those in a "tougher spot" than us because we know God's grace is the only difference. We share in the benefits of grace as benefactors of grace. And so the adventure begins.

Nuggets from this Chapter

- Grace not only flows to us, it flows through us.
- Dismissing our own depravity by comparing it to the depravity of others cheapens our understanding of grace.
- Having received grace, God's design is that we give it away as we live among others in need of grace.
- When we see Jesus, we see grace. When we see grace, we see love. When we see love, we see the Father.
- The benefits of grace equip us for purpose as we walk out our lives here and now.

Chapter 3

THE JOY OF WINNING

Criminal defendants, especially first-time offenders, often don't understand everything that happens during their trial or hearing. Some don't even know if they've won or lost their case after the final gavel rap. On the occasions I won criminal cases, I would head out of the courtroom with my client as quickly as possible. I wanted to explain to them in the relative privacy of the courthouse hallway what happened. There were several reasons for my hasty exit, the least not being I didn't want to risk seeming to gloat in front of the judge or prosecutor. That was just bad form.

On one such occasion, as I prompted my client to follow me out of the courtroom, he immediately began asking, "What happened?" Even as I told him I would explain outside, he persisted, "What happened? What happened? Did we win? Did we win?"

"Yes, we won," I said, keeping my voice un-gloatingly low as we made our way up the aisle toward the door. Right there in the middle of the aisle, walking from the bench to the hallway, unable to contain himself at the good news of victory, he started to celebrate. Part of his celebration was an attempt to grab and hug me. I put him off with a decisive correction of "No hugging." Of course, once we got outside, I explained how and why we won.

His brash celebration came from his realization of freedom and the value he now placed on that freedom, having recently faced the real prospect of losing it. Those three little words, "Yes, we won" led to an outburst of gratitude and relief almost resulting in an awkward bear-hug moment in an un-bear-hug-friendly setting. This defendant experienced the thrill of being declared "not guilty" even though he was, in fact, guilty. We won on a valid legal point, but he had broken the law—and he knew it. He felt the joy of escaping punishment despite his guilt.

The freedom Christ won for us is far more than escaping punishment. His sacrificial death offered a valid legal substitute for our guilt, and we get a "not guilty" verdict that should have us dancing in the aisles. Our joy should be uncontainable. We should throw our arms around the One who won our freedom in endless gratitude. Unlike my reaction to the joyful defendant, Jesus hugs us back.

Christ's death and resurrection won us more than we realize with benefits greater than we imagine. Experiencing our new freedom in concrete ways evokes "inexpressible and glorious joy" (1 Peter 1:8) as we live it out, but living the promise of abundant life Jesus paid for depends on receiving and sharing His grace.

The only way to receive grace is by acknowledging we need grace. We acknowledge our need when we admit our faults to others and ourselves. The realization and multiplication of grace happens when we unite with others to bring things into the light we might prefer to hide in the darkness. The framework for the covenant of grace Jesus invites us into is found in 2 Corinthians 3:6–18,[2] where the Apostle Paul contrasts the Old Covenant of Moses (the law) and the New Covenant of Jesus (grace).

The ministry of Moses was of the law and the law brought death. It's the ministry of condemnation as no one can adequately keep the law. No matter that it was the ministry of guilt and death, there was a measure of glory associated with it. That glory, however, was fading and infinitely insignificant compared to the now-available glory of the New Covenant of Jesus.

Life under the Old Covenant is one of insecurity and despair as we try to do the undoable. There's no boldness in living, since keeping the law is impossible and every attempt must be veiled to hide our failures. Even as we hide behind rules and performance, we're aware of our limitations. We know we can't maintain the pretense forever. Between our fear of failure and maneuvering to keep others from seeing the depravity that invariably reveals itself, we're always tending our insecurity—and it's exhausting.

The Covenant of Jesus brings a never-fading glory. It's the eternal glory of Jesus living in us. His Spirit in us satisfies the requirements of the law by His righteousness with no effort on our part. His indwelling is all we need for good standing with the Father, and we live in the boldness for which He created and called us. We don't have to hide anymore. We finally can rest.

There are two options for life: law or grace. They present a choice, not a combination. There's no "Law-Grace Combo Option" for our inadequate attempts at performance when we want to enhance our chance of acceptance. Either we choose the self-reliant performance woven into the Law of Moses, or we accept the satisfaction of the law through the grace and sacrifice of Jesus.

Human nature pulls us toward the default position of keeping rules because—believe it or not—it's easier for our flesh than relying on the finished work of Christ. Our flesh craves the tangible. It takes conscious effort to deny its innate bent toward score keeping. The letter of the law is what we point to as evidence of our self-provided righteousness. At the end of the day, we place a star in the box, measure our performance and judge ourselves good. Or not.

Our flesh pulls us to perform though we know we can't pull it off. It produces shame and fear of exposure and conceals us behind Moses' veil to hide the limitations of our soul, creating or reinforcing walls between us and God, us and other people, or both. Such walls stem the flow of grace.

We can't enjoy the freedom of the New Covenant while striving to keep the Old. Energy meant for bold living gets spent struggling to hide behind the veil, and the covenant of Moses breeds insecurity from the certain knowledge we will fail and someone will actually see us. That insecurity results in prideful self-promotion as we try to hide our limitations.

Insecurity shows up as boastful arrogance or timid fear, both outward manifestations of pride. God never offers to meet us in our pride. In fact, He actively opposes a posture of pride: *"God opposes the proud but shows favor to the humble"* (James 4:6). Our only hope is choosing the covenant Jesus offers, which means dropping the veil in humility to allow for our flaws. Our performance behind Moses' veil puts us on display. Our flaws revealed on the grace side of the veil put Jesus on display. His glory shines.

Accepting the invitation into a life of grace-only is liberating and powerful. Sold out to the truth that we are "good enough" only by the gift of righteousness through faith in Jesus, we can stop trying to preserve the charade of our perfection. We can stop pretending in order to throw religious folks off the scent of our depravity. We can be about the true transformation of our souls.

Freedom is born from grace that lets us drop the veil to live authentically with others. They get to see us; really see us. Not everyone we know needs access to the closed closets and dark crawl spaces of our souls. However, for those with whom we have time-tested relationships, we foster transparency for the ongoing transformation that results in greater liberty.

Admitting our weaknesses and imperfections, we become strong and perfect in Jesus. His grace never blinks at our depravity but meets us eternally with redemption. He embraces us and removes our limitations so we walk in His fullness. From the realization of His grace, we know love; we know the Father through the Son.

The grace of Jesus wins us a "not guilty" verdict and removes the need for any effort on our part to defend ourselves. It frees us to live boldly in the assurance of acceptance. It delivers us from the prospect of an eternity exiled from the Kingdom and instead allows us direct access to the King. Grace redeems the limitations of our humanity and affords us relationship with the Creator of the universe.

Nuggets from this Chapter

- The New Covenant requires transparency about our flaws while the Old Covenant required hiding behind adherence to laws.
- Many "Christians" are living an Old Covenant version of Christianity, which isn't Christianity at all.
- Admitting our faults in humility puts Jesus and His grace on display for others that need to know Him.
- Where we attempt to be perceived as righteous by the law, death and condemnation are given priority over life and grace.
- Insecurity is the result of faulty efforts we foster to make ourselves look good compared to the law.
- Receiving and sharing grace is the key to the abundant life Jesus promises.
- Grace frees us to live boldly as heirs of the Kingdom.

Chapter 4

OUR NEW REALITY

The Good News of Jesus is better than we realize. We don't have to die and go to heaven to experience all the benefits His life, death and resurrection paid for. He invites us to step into the benefits of His sacrifice as early and as often as we are willing. Through Him, we are *"heirs of God and co-heirs with Christ."*[3] Jesus died to secure our inheritance. He rose again to hand it to us. The abundant benefits of the Kingdom are available to us by His grace here and now, not delayed until the beginning of eternity in heaven. Eternity begins today.

What constrains us from running in the abundant life He bought for us are the common conditions into which we're born. They are the limitations of our humanity. Left to our own devices, there's a limit to how fast and far we will go. The capacity of our destiny depends on our acknowledging and exchanging these constraints. Constraints we are willing to exchange become multipliers of our potential.

Jesus came to cure our common condition. Referencing a prophecy recorded in Isaiah 53:4,[4] Matthew 8:17 says Jesus *"took up our infirmities and bore our diseases."*

The words "bore" and "took" mean He receives them from us—but not passively.

The word for "took" in this verse comes from the original word, *lambano*.[5] It's a word of action that means specifically "to lay hold by aggressively (actively) accepting what is available (offered)."[6] "Took" isn't passive; it's the assertive action of the Receiver to obtain what's offered. This detailed and distinct meaning is important in understanding the redemption of our limitations and (as we'll see later) the appropriation of God's grace.

Jesus never hesitates. He reaches out and eagerly grabs hold of our limitations as soon as we offer them up. He takes our constraints and exchanges them for the fullness available through Him. We don't have to accept the limitations inherent in our human condition when we depend on the grace of Jesus.

"Infirmities" and "diseases" seem similar but are very different in this instance. Disease, as used here, means sickness and primarily indicates a problem with our body that results in pain or restrictions. It's the flu or maybe something more chronic that sends you to the doctor's office.

Infirmities are something else. In Matthew 8:17, "infirmities" refers to the limitations of our soul. Our soul consists of our mind, will and emotions. The limitations of our soul are shortcomings of capacity in one or more of these parts of our self. These infirmities became part of our soul's DNA when Adam and Eve first sinned in the Garden of Eden. We're all born with them and until we're born again are destined to live within their constraints.

Sick or injured, our body can't physically accomplish the same things it can when it is healed and whole. Capacity is limited. The same is true for our soul. Just as a long-distance runner with a ruptured Achilles tendon can run neither fast nor far, the infirmities referred to in Matthew 8:17 are limitations of our soul that keep us from running passionately the race of life before us.

The definition of the original word translated "infirmities"[7] refers to four specific inborn limitations of our soul. These limitations of our soul are listed specifically in the definition. They are:

- Our ability to restrain ourselves from our own depravity or "corrupt desires";
- Our ability to persevere through "trials and troubles";
- Our ability to understand;
- And our ability to do "great and glorious" things.[8]

If you consider them for just a minute, you will agree that you have experienced limitations in your abilities in each of the areas above. While there are things you understand, trials you have persevered through and corrupt desires you have been able to overcome, there are times you haven't accomplished those things as well. There are also dreams and visions of great and glorious things you carry which convince you that you are here for "more." Those dreams are real, even if they are buried, and your ability to overcome your limitations to achieve the fullness of your design is attainable.

Getting Back What Was Lost

As children of the first Adam, we come to this world bound by these four limitations of our soul. An honest assessment reveals even after our second birth these limitations persist to some degree. That honest assessment is vital. We must acknowledge our limitations before Jesus can redeem them and we can enjoy the benefit of Him taking them. You can't exchange what you don't realize or admit you possess. Eyes to see the limitations we have settled for allow us to own them and exchange them for the restoration of our original design.

When Adam and Eve rebelled in the Garden, they did not physically die, despite God's warning of certain death if they ate from the forbidden tree. Their physical life beyond their rebellion did not make God a liar. There was death, just not the falling down, stop breathing kind. The death they experienced was far worse.

The spirit at the center of their being, which was God's spirit within them, ceased to be their Source of life. The Life the Father breathed into them to make them living creatures in His image was instantly gone. Adam and Eve—and all their descendants—were left with the soul of an orphan exiled from the presence of the Father.

The response of the orphan soul is always, "What must I *do* to take care of myself?" Orphans demand control over the outcome of their efforts because they are unable to trust they will ever receive anything not acquired via their *doing* something. Unless we are born again into the Kingdom of our Father, we perpetually look for ways to earn approval and gain access.

Jesus came to restore the living breath of God within us. When we are born again, a new creation from the inside out, we welcome His grace to restore us to the Father. The realization of our adoption through His grace affords us the rights, privileges, benefits and favor of sons and daughters. We are heirs through Christ, co-heirs with Him. Even so, we often battle orphan soul behavior and continue in self-exile from a King and Kingdom that invite us in.

The limitations of our soul show up when our will takes priority over God's Spirit in our choices. Adam and Eve, in effect, killed the Father's Spirit within them to allow their souls to rule. Jesus paid the price for that rebellion, and we have the opportunity, through Him, to put our soul to death and allow His Spirit to reign within us. His Spirit has no infirmities.

Most of us realize our design toward greater things even when evidence of that purpose is not immediately evident in our present circumstances. The restraint of desire for the sake of practical responsibility versus unleashed passion toward fulfillment of a legitimate great and glorious purpose creates in us a drive that propels us forward. That drive to run as fast as possible towards the finish line is like the heart of a champion Thoroughbred racehorse. It's powerful and passionate as it pushes us toward our ultimate goal and it's a legitimate part of our design. It's the way God intends the zealous playing out of a powerful Kingdom.

Taking the Bit

Thoroughbred racehorses are bred to be fast and to be passionate about speed, but they aren't born knowing how to race. Thoroughbred foals know instinctively they can run. Within the first few hours of life, they are up and running. The same instinct that makes them passionate about running makes them resist the very things that can transform them from a stallion to a champion: the control of the reins and the weight of a rider.

Before even the most meticulously bred horse can race, it has to learn to accept the fundamental piece of training gear, the bit. The bit sits in the horse's mouth and attaches to the reins. A horse's first reaction to the bit is to spit it out. It feels unnatural.

To coax a horse to open its mouth and take the bit, an experienced trainer keeps a stash of sugar cubes in their pocket. Horses clamber after the sweetness of the sugar and eagerly open their mouths for more. Not only does the sugar get the horse to open its mouth, it creates excess saliva, which makes the bit more comfortable. After a while, the trainer no longer tempts the horse with sugar cubes. It willingly opens its mouth for the bit because it's learned to trust the one holding the reins.

The reins let the rider guide the horse, restrain it when necessary and permit it to run with abandon when the time is right. In the hands of a skillful rider, the reins exert the control necessary to draw out the promise of the champion within. If a horse won't take the bit it will never fulfill its potential, no matter how impressive its pedigree, how powerful its heart and legs or how passionately it runs.

Meekness is harnessed strength. It's the redirection of otherwise powerful but out-of-control intentions toward a legitimate purpose. It's capturing the complete potential through limiting the time and direction of application at the hand and discretion of another.

Harnessing our potential toward a destiny makes that destiny attainable. It's not about how fast or far we can run by ourselves, but yielding control to realize our full potential. It's exchanging the constraints of our humanity for the limitlessness of His loving restraint. It requires the discomfort of a bit we resist until tasting His goodness (Psalm 34:8).[9]

The difference between a stallion and a champion is the ability to actualize potential. The immature stallion must accept the harnessing of their potential to realize their destiny. The realization of grace in our lives depends on repentance (changing of our minds) in order to enjoy the benefits.

Stallions are wild with no other options for their provision, protection or place than to fend for themselves. Champions are cared for and their place is provided. They know their place is assured because of Whose they are as much as because of who they are.

Redeeming the Circles

In college, I joined a fraternity. Once a year, alumni and undergraduates of this group gathered for a pig roast. At one point during the roast, all the men would form a circle and because of the way God wired me, I was equipped, therefore chosen, to deliver a speech of sorts to that circle of drunken pig roasters. I would stand in the circle and share words meant to instill a sense of community and vision for the group, albeit rooted in carnal, temporary ideas of what community and vision actually were.

As an adult, part of my ministry involves serving on and leading "Quest" events where groups of men go away to purposefully pursue the heart of God. Upon returning from these Quests, the men form a circle for a final charge, and I encourage them to walk out the victory revealed during their time away.

The words I speak now carry the weight of truth, the longevity of eternity and the promise of the Word not returning void. The grace of Jesus redeemed the gift and ability that were part of my design once applied to something as temporal as a fraternity's pig roast and now harnesses them to realize their eternal intent in agreement with God's purposes.

God wants to redeem all things, and in His grace takes the limitations of our soul in exchange for the benefits of His purposes for us. For every limitation we face, redemption is available through the grace of Jesus. We exchange our flawed applications of ability for the multiplication of His grace and enjoy the benefits that exceed anything we can accomplish on our own.

Romans 5:17[10] says that through Jesus we are able to *"reign in life."* Reigning is our new reality, but what does that mean? How do we know if we are actually living the truth of that Biblical promise?

To help answer those questions, consider this definition: I know I am reigning in life when I understand things, restrain myself from corrupt desires, persevere through trials and do great and glorious things. The reality of reigning in life is enjoying victory and fullness in each of these areas. You can and you do because He meant it when He said it.

Nuggets from this Chapter

- We are born into the legacy of Adam that leaves us limited in body and soul (i.e., our mind, will and emotions).
- Limitations of our soul prevent righteous living, perseverance, understanding and accomplishing our intended destiny.
- Jesus takes the limitations we inherit as fallen people as we willingly hand them over.
- The exchange of those limitations for the fullness of God's original design is available in the grace of Jesus.
- Our full potential manifests when we yield control to the Father's direction and design.
- Grace allows us to relinquish control and exchange our finite abilities for His infinite possibilities.

Chapter 5
RESTRAINING OUR DEPRAVITY

There was a time as an adult when I made plans to meet a friend from college at a football game. Before the game, someone told me this friend had expressed some apprehension about our meeting. Some business associates would be at the game with him, and he was concerned I might embarrass him. The realization that my past life's behavior left such a lasting and obviously bad impression shook me up. For a second the thought that I could have ever been that person made me feel like—well, like a fraud.

Later at the game, I watched people behave much as I used to, and I literally cringed at the thought that I was "that guy." How in the world did things ever get so off track? As I saw through new eyes my old self in those carousing at the game, it was embarrassing. I understood my friend's misgivings. At the same time, the temptation to feel I was a fraud crept back in. Am I really different and credible now given I was so "not" back then?

The next day as I shared these thoughts and feelings with a friend, he reminded me of the victory of grace evident in my life. He reminded me of the ongoing redemption

I live every day. Together, we gave thanks that the grace of Jesus continues to replace my depravity with His glory. I wept as I considered the indescribable goodness of His transforming love. I wept as I appreciated that I'm not stuck "there" any longer.

The answer to my question about my credibility is yes. Yes, I am different, not because of any feat I've accomplished, but because the grace of Jesus redeems my inability to restrain my depravity. His grace appropriated "crucifies" my old self and destroys the power of sin in my life. Best of all, His grace allows me to allow Him to live through me.[11]

If I were still living my old pattern of corruption, the consequences would be too many to count. Since through grace I crucified the person I was and now allow Christ to live in me, my life bears the fruit of its new landscape: love, joy, peace and hope. Now there is life and life more abundant. There's nothing fraudulent about that.

Grace to Overcome

No matter how hard we try or how well intentioned we are, we simply will never reach a point where our "goodness" exceeds our depravity. We are born into a state that dooms us to a fallen nature. The new-birth transformation available through the sacrifice of Jesus allows Him to shape and change us. He is the Source.

Our transformation is by Him, through Him and from Him. Only He can get us there, not us trying to show Him how we can get there for Him or ahead of Him.

When we've had enough of our depraved choices and their consequences, the invitation stands. We can look up and see the way Jesus made for us, submitting ourselves to Him and the benefits of His sacrifice. The longer we wait, however, the more difficult the consequences.

Consequences come as a result of our choices and the fallen state of man. The difficulty of those consequences aren't evidence of an angry God; they are a contrast to the kindness of the Lord that lead us to repentance. Jesus is not mad at us. He's not punishing us; He loves us enough to let us choose.

The promise that forms the foundation of our hope is that by God's grace we can overcome the limitations of our fallen nature. The grace Jesus offers equips us to rise above the rebellion in our soul that battles the truth of His spirit within us. That's why He said His "yoke" (teaching) is "easy" and "light" (Matthew 11:28–30).[12] The teaching He brings is not a burden of performance, but instead it is an invitation into forgiveness that comes with His satisfaction of justice. It's easy and light because He's doing the heavy lifting. He died because we can never be "good enough." The result is we receive. Receiving should be easy.

To receive freedom, we simply have to agree with His grace. We inherit more than we deserve, not earn more than we have. Less is more and giving up gets us everything. The more we try to prove our freedom or accomplish our ministry, the more we push against the grace of Jesus.

Only Two Kingdoms

In John 2, we read how Jesus cleared the shopkeepers and moneychangers out of the Temple, reminding His disciples of the prophetic promise that *"Zeal for your house will consume me"* (John 2:17; Psalm 69:9). Jesus cleansed the temple by chasing out the loan sharks and merchants who'd set up shop to make a few dollars off the pilgrims who'd traveled to Jerusalem for Passover.

We are now God's Temple as His Spirit dwells at the deepest, most profound parts of our being, our holy of holies, if you will. Our soul exists in intimate proximity to His Spirit, in the Holy Place of our identity. How zealous are we to chase out the unsavory visitors—or long-term residents—who have made their way into our soul, often by way of our invitations? Do we express our displeasure with a passing scowl, then turn our backs and pretend they're no longer there?

If you know Jesus as your Savior, He has come to dwell in you as His Temple and has changed your identity at your core. You are righteous and holy in that place where He dwells, but it's clear for most of us not everything that comes out of us is at all righteous or holy. It seems there are some lingering merchants with some of their wares still trespassing in God's Temple. Even after we chase them out with a whip, there may be some trace of them. It may just be the smell of the animals or a few scattered pieces of silver, but to finish the quest before us, it all has to go.

I have a friend who once was in the middle of a battle with addiction and I was describing to him the possibilities of victory in Jesus. I was explaining the depth of healing and freedom I found in Jesus and telling him those were available to him, too. As we spoke, my friend said, "I believe that, but what does it cost?" I hesitated and considered the question before answering, "Everything."

Even I was a bit shocked at the weight of the answer. I admit I'd never really considered the question or the answer in practical terms, where life was in the middle of the dialogue. Sure, I knew the idea was right from Bible studies or sermons or whatever, but this was heavier than just an idea. This was the realization that "everything" meant everything. Your whole life if you want His.

We can't intentionally dabble in depravity and get away with it. There are only two kingdoms; we don't get to invent a third. It's all or nothing and the middle ground will get you killed.

> *"Search me, God, and know my heart; test me and know my anxious thoughts. See if there is any offensive way in me, and lead me in the way everlasting"* (Psalm 139: 23–24*)*.

The original word translated in Psalm 139 as "offensive"[13] includes "pain, sorrow" and in some forms "idol." The prayer of Psalm 139, then, is for God to search us and reveal any painful, sorrowful or idolatrous ways within. Understanding the deeper meaning of this prayer, we gain greater insight into the function of our soul.

Where there is wickedness in our behaviors, there is a reason for it. Our bad choices are the result of pain and sorrow in our broken soul. As we examine our depraved ways and ask the Lord to show us, He often will lead us to a lie fostered in pain and sorrow we've experienced. Somewhere along the way, something hurt us, and we believed a lie that led us to self-protect from getting hurt again.

Sometimes the lie is about us: "I deserved to be hurt." Sometimes the lie is about God: "He caused this" or "He let this happen." Sometimes the lie is about both: "God was right to let me be hurt/to hurt me. It's what I deserve." Bad choices spring from lies such as these, and set us on a path of repeated depravity. The good news is if we discover the hurt, God can heal it.

We fall into the sin of idolatry when we believe a lie that comes from a wound and promote ourselves to god over that area of our lives. We reject the protection and provision of God and determine that we are better equipped to rule in that area. Unwilling to risk the vulnerability of being hurt again, we self-protect, reasoning we can control pain-causing circumstances better than He did. The result is increasingly depraved choices and difficult consequences. The spiral of depravity has begun.

"Search me, God" will take us as deep as we are willing to go. If we'll trust Him to show us, He will not only exchange His will for ours, but He'll heal the hurt that led us to the place of making ourselves idols over those areas of our lives in the first place.

The Best Deal We'll Ever Get

In historical land battles, those locked in combat with the enemy had two choices: Hunker down indefinitely in their foxholes in hopes the adversary would inexplicably retreat, or when given the command, emerge and charge forward with life-or-death ferocity to take ground from the enemy. Once out of the foxhole, there was no turning back. It was all or nothing and stopping even for a moment's second-guessing between the foxhole and the fight was almost certain death as indecision exposed vulnerability.

Failing to own your sin is hiding in your foxhole, refusing to face the all-or-nothing battle for your freedom raging all around you. Stopping short of total victory as you cling to those behaviors you can justify or mitigate as "not all that bad" doesn't work. Either option is a sure way to maintain sinful patterns of behavior, and in doing so, settle for less than complete victory. You can't exchange what you continue to hold onto.

The good news is we win. It's already decided and finished; Jesus said so. He paid for it, and we inherit it. Our part is to receive. However, we won't receive things we don't realize are paid for, and we won't cash in if we value other things more. If we choose not to walk out of our depravity, Jesus loves us enough to let us continue to slop around in it, with the warning that the consequences will eventually kill us if we don't change our mind (1 Corinthians 5:5).[14]

Jesus is absolutely the best deal any one of us can ever imagine. He wants to pay the price, offer the benefits, grant the understanding and fuel the purpose. He wants to fill us and flow from us and all we have to do is be us. Even the worst part of us doesn't run Him off; in fact, it's the darkest places of our lives where His glory shines brightest.

Nuggets from this Chapter

- By grace, Jesus replaces our depravity with His glory.
- We walk in freedom from depravity through an all-or-nothing exchange of our life for His.
- We can't exchange what we first won't take hold of.
- Ignoring or rationalizing corrupt behaviors keeps us enslaved to those behaviors.
- Revealing lies born from pain opens the door to healing and stops the cycle of depravity.
- God's grace allows us to allow Him to live through us.

Chapter 6
PERSEVERING THROUGH TRIALS

It's common for people facing criminal charges to plead sincerely for mercy in a court of law. They tell the judge they've learned the error of their ways and vow that they would never do "it" again. And they mean it. Everything in them says the anguish they're experiencing as they face the consequences of their crime is too painful to submit to again. As a result, they plead for mercy with untainted conviction that leniency is not only reasonable but also wise.

Of course, the court is obligated to view each case with neutrality and temper mercy with justice. The judge can fully believe the defendant's sincere regret but still appropriately exact a difficult ruling of imposed punishment to close the case.

The trials we face, because of our own bad choices or circumstances beyond our control, demand perseverance to develop the character required for this life of adventure. We have to persevere through the point of pain if we're going to grow in our patience to walk through future hardships. Unlike defendants subject to the court's rule, we often have opportunity to stop our pain early.

Declaring our current trial a mistrial so we can flee the courtroom and escape present and predicted pain produces an incomplete measure of development. We choose immediate comfort at the cost of a missed opportunity for growth and advancement toward our goal. The lack of a fuller measure of growth is failure within failure.

Grace gets us through. It empowers us to endure hardships through the fullest measure of their consequences. On the other side of the pain, we experience the advantages of increased endurance, strengthened character and ultimately mature faith.

A prerequisite to gaining the wisdom and knowledge we need to continue our quest is single-mindedness in pursuing them. If we're double-minded, we'll bail out at the first sign of trouble, usually after taking a beating but without the benefit of growth. Once we bail out, the possibility of growth is gone. To stand through the storm requires deliberate steadfastness that sees beyond the immediate hardship.

It's not easy to stare into the coming storm, already feeling the wind and rain of the outer bands, and decide intentionally to face it head on. Once the difficulty has begun, the decision to endure is ours. Knowing the storm will make a way for the Light of a new day to shine through us brighter than before is the grace that allows us to persevere in increasing measure.

Set Your Face Like Flint

The only way to reach the fullness of our design and release the champion within is to persevere through trials, setbacks, challenges and even apparent catastrophe. It's the only way. There are times we're going to take hits, maybe hard ones, and the only thing we can do is make up our mind to keep going. In this life we are going to have trouble (John 16:33).[15] The grace of Jesus allows us to persevere through trouble because He did.

Isaiah 50:6–7 tells us of Jesus persevering:

"I offered my back to those who beat me, my cheeks to those who pulled out my beard; I did not hide my face from mocking and spitting. Because the Sovereign Lord helps me, I will not be disgraced. Therefore have I set my face like flint, and I know I will not be put to shame."

On the way to His death, Jesus set His *"face like flint."* That's what He offers us as redemption for our limited capacity to persevere. He knows the pain of the trials we face (Hebrews 4:15),[16] and no matter how difficult things are in the moment, they don't exceed what He did for us (Hebrews 12:3–4).[17]

In setting His face like flint, He bought us the perseverance available through His grace. We persevere by appropriating what He has made available by grace.

We are invited to eternal glory beyond inevitable suffering (2 Corinthians 4:17).[18] When we understand the invitation and say "Yes" even before we know the details of the coming storm, by His grace we set our face like flint to walk from glory to glory in freedom.

Grace to See

> *"Where there is no prophetic vision the people cast off restraint, but blessed is he who keeps the law"* (Proverbs 29:18 ESV).

If we can't see things from the perspective of how God intends them, we'll increasingly walk away from Him and choose our own way. We won't make it. It's revelation of what He desires for us and is inviting us into that allows us to persevere by the grace of Jesus.

We can't see as God sees if we don't know Him. We can't know Him if we don't spend time with Him. Jesus' perseverance described above in Isaiah 50 above didn't start with His suffering. It started with spending time with His Father. In verses 4 and 5 preceding the prophetic suffering of Christ, Isaiah writes

> *"The Sovereign Lord has given me a well-instructed tongue, to know the word that sustains*

the weary. He wakens me morning by morning, wakens my ear to listen like one being instructed. The Sovereign Lord has opened my ears; I have not been rebellious, I have not turned away."

The Son shows us the way. It starts with waking *"morning by morning"* with the Father. We take on His perspective by spending time with Him and studying His Word. With God's perspective comes His vision for our lives, and with His vision we can set our eyes and intentions beyond our immediate challenges and press through the problems to reach the destination.

Problems persist as long as we live in a fallen world; nothing is ever going to be completely satisfactory. The distraction of problems takes us off course from our intended destiny. We need to see to persevere and we need to persevere to realize God's intentions for our lives. Without vision, we won't make it.

There is glory beyond the suffering. Jesus could see and He endured to realize the glory of His destiny. Hebrews 12:1(b)–2 tells us to *"look to Jesus, the founder and perfecter of our faith, who for the joy that was set before him endured the cross, despising the shame, and is seated at the right hand of the throne of God"* (ESV).

Catching a vision of the Kingdom and the glory intended for sons and daughters of God to carry on earth as it is in heaven, we persevere. We need prophetic vision for the appropriate restraint. Sometimes that restraint is to keep us from running ahead of God's plan. Sometimes it's to keep us from running away from God's plan. With restraint, we'll endure the suffering of perseverance and we'll benefit from the development of our character. That prepares us for promotion.

Fresh vision is like a deep, cleansing breath. When you see what God is doing and wants to do in you, all the foolishness that threatens your destiny appears insignificant. With a glimpse of the finish line, you become tolerant of the intolerable for the sake of the eternal.

When you reach a point where you have no hope in your circumstances, ask to see. When God shows you what He's doing and commissions you to be part of it, the volume of the call drowns out the lies of the trials. Agreeing with the truth, obedience becomes second nature as revelation breeds new nature that agrees with God's nature. From that new perspective, the distractions of trouble take their rightful place as irrelevant compared to the call of glory.

Joy from Perseverance

Life is hard and change is challenging. The difficulty of life has gotten on and in every one of us to some degree. The opportunity to redeem those things that affect us negatively for the promise of glory takes time; time requires perseverance and perseverance holds a promise.

> *"Blessed is the man who remains steadfast under trial, for when he has stood the test he will receive the crown of life, which God has promised to those who love him"* (James 1:12).

A crown represents honor and reward. It's a metaphor for eternal blessing.[19] The *"crown of life"* is the promised life of John 10:10 as well as John 3:16.[20] The honor and reward of perseverance are life both abundant and eternal. God promises us the reward (crown) of life when we push through hard places. Hard places pepper every road worth traveling. There is eternal reward that is available in increasing measure as we persevere, but we have to stay the course to discover the treasure.

The decisions we make to keep going don't come from our discipline. Our discipline comes from our love for God and our love for God comes from Him: *"We love because he first loved us"* (1 John 4:19). As we receive His love, we love Him back. Loving Him back, we choose Him despite the trials that test that love.

Crowns are blessings and crowns are life. We get both from loving Him who first loved us. In Revelation 4:10–11[21] John tells of his vision of *"twenty-four elders"* kneeling before Jesus in heaven, laying their crowns at His feet as they say *"You are worthy, our Lord and God, to receive glory and honor and power."* That's a perfect picture of what we do in life as well as what we will do in eternity.

Because God loves us, we love Him back. We receive life both abundant and eternal as His love and grace push us through the hard places, and then we give that life and all its blessings back to Him.

The End Game

Pushing through the hard places is much more difficult than walking roads of depravity grounded in selfishness. Having walked such roads in my past, I know that the parties and selfishness require little sacrifice as comfort and enjoyment are the treasure. I also know adventures on such roads are temporal and shallow and last only as long as the beer doesn't run out.

The road that leads to treasure is rich and forever and difficult. It's the only path that satisfies the longing of our soul to be part of something beyond what we can see and foresee. The adventure of a life worth dying for requires sacrificing selfishness every day. That sacrifice never becomes easy; it just becomes more natural. That is, our nature changes.

Blessings from living a life of loving Him aren't the end game. Life isn't even the end game. The end game is Him. The end game is Jesus walking and talking on this earth today through us. The end game is He gets the glory. Everything else is just a bonus. Jesus gives His life for ours, and we give it back to Him by surrendering our will to His. Doing so, we join Him in His quest to redeem His world.

Grace makes it possible for us to persevere through trials and sets in motion the beautiful cycle that starts with receiving His love and results in us laying our "crowns" at His feet. It starts and ends with Him at the cost of me. As upside-down and backward as that is from the world's way of thinking, that's where happiness resides and the party never ends.

Nuggets from this Chapter

- Where we step towards the Lord, there are challenges that mature and develop us.
- There are no promises of ease or comfort in the Kingdom of God.
- Grace gives us vision for where the Lord is calling us so we can persevere through the trials that come in our development.
- Where we persevere, the pain of the trials gives way to the joy of the glory.
- We are called from glory to glory, and that call

presents a choice. With fresh vision for new glory, grace empowers us to step from the comfort of the former glory to the unknown of the new glory.

Chapter 7
UNDERSTANDING THINGS

One morning I set aside several hours to worship, read the Bible, write and pray. I cleared the calendar and was alone in an empty house with nothing to do but pursue the Lord. I invested significant, intentional time to create an atmosphere that was peaceful and reverent. Here's what happened: nothing. I didn't have any earth-moving realization of God's presence, nor did I understand better the struggles I was facing that sent me earnestly seeking Him that day.

In the coming days, however, I saw the value of the morning's investment. God started to meet me in the questions I presented and the frustrations I wrestled. He began to shine light on the way He saw things and to direct me ever so gently toward my next steps. He subtly revealed Himself and I began to gain a heavenly understanding of my earthly circumstances. Shape by shape, revelation by revelation, the puzzle started to take form.

God is not interested in being our genie in a bottle or in performing "magic tricks" for us to remedy our circumstances. Instead, as we walk with Him, He helps us from the relational experience, not the snap of His fingers. We increase in wisdom through intimacy until the need for resolution to specific situations fades to insignificant compared to the glory of His presence.

Proverbs 25:2 says, *"It is the glory of God to conceal a matter; to search out a matter is the glory of kings."*

God glories in concealment because it draws us into deeper relationship with Him as it calls out our royal identity. The pursuit hints at romance and adventure as we courageously venture deeper into relationship with an all-powerful God. It's the epic nature of this relational "dance" that provides the heavenly backdrop to our time on earth.

The seeking out of the concealed matters of God works out our inner king or queen. Pursuing the King who designed us requires us to walk as His royal children. Not to over-simplify, but it's much like the eternal application of the schoolyard taunt, "It takes one to know one." As we engage in seeking out the hidden treasures of a Royal King, we awaken in us what we find in Him. We begin to see from a royal perspective and experience the benefit grace affords us to truly understanding things.

How to Understand

The raw material for wisdom is knowledge, but it's more than the accumulation of information. Knowledge becomes wisdom through the experiences we allow, and we "allow" experiences by saying "Yes" to the invitations of God to go from one glory to the next.

The "how to" is usually the thing we want to know next. The Apostle Paul touches on the "how to" of life in the first chapter of Ephesians. He is writing to people he loves and in whom he as has invested himself. He tells them he's praying for them to receive the *"Spirit of wisdom and revelation."* He's praying for them to get the "how to."

- **The Spirit:** The "how to" is in and depends on Holy Spirit. We receive Him; we don't work to impress Him in hopes He'll somehow reward us. He provides the wisdom and revelation necessary for walking out the life of an heir.

- **Revelation:** Invitations into greater maturity, wisdom and understanding come by revelation. There must be prophetic insight into where God is calling you to agree with Him. There has to be relationship with the Counselor to receive the counsel. Revelation is when you read a verse and the one-hundredth time you read it is when it suddenly comes alive for you personally—just as Jeremiah 29:11 did for me—and then living it.

- **Wisdom:** We obtain wisdom by agreeing with God in the things He is calling us into, even as those things often take us to uncomfortable circumstances. Our character matures in those challenging circumstances. Wisdom is the application of knowledge coupled with the depth of experience and is as dependent on our character as it is our education. Character grows through perseverance, and perseverance requires trials. The accumulation of wisdom typically depends on experiencing discomfort.

Understanding isn't knowledge, although knowledge is necessary to understand. The benefit of grace which affords us the ability to understand things requires wisdom and revelation. Those who worship in spirit and truth receive and live in wisdom and revelation.

The Spirit, knowledge, wisdom and revelation all are necessary to understanding. If we treat knowledge as the goal, memorizing Scripture and learning doctrine without wisdom and revelation, pride takes over. Knowledge begs for the company of wisdom and revelation because revelation illuminates knowledge and wisdom applies it. Knowledge, then, is the fuel for wisdom and revelation and therefore, the fuel for walking in spirit and truth.

Think of wisdom being horizontal and revelation being vertical. Wisdom is living among other people and circumstances. We can see, touch and feel the application of wisdom. Wisdom shows up in the things we do and their accompanying results. Revelation is Spirit to spirit. It's the open conduit between heaven and earth. It's community with the invisible yet relational God of the universe.

If we depend only on truth and knowledge, those things we can learn and master, we will dry up. There's limited life in things we can control. We reject the breath of God when we limit our relationship to things we can learn *about* Him. If that happens, sooner or later, to some degree, we beat people up with our limited understanding.

If we depend on only spirit and revelation without the foundation of the Word of God for wisdom and truth, we'll be off-kilter and open to error. God speaks—I'm sure of it—but He's speaking for His glory, not our ministry.

Let It Kill You

In John 4, Jesus meets a Samaritan woman at a well and asks her for a drink of water. In the conversation they have after she recovers from her shock that a Jewish man spoke to her, Jesus reveals a coming change in the "how to" of humanity's perception of worship. In doing so, He shows us how to activate the benefit of grace of "understanding a thing."

> *"...believe me, a time is coming when you will worship the Father neither on this mountain nor*

> *in Jerusalem…a time is coming and has now come when the true worshipers will worship the Father in the Spirit and in truth, for they are the kind of worshipers the Father seeks. God is spirit, and his worshipers must worship in the Spirit and in truth"* (v. 21, 23–24).

Pre-Jesus, acceptable worship took place only at certain places and times and in very specific ways. Ever the revolutionary, Jesus declares things are about to change and that change includes the sacred ways of worship. Worshipping in spirit and truth meant worship wouldn't be confined to a place, a day or a ritual. This was a huge shift from where things were, and it's a shift from where many Christians to this day hang out to this day.

Jesus wasn't talking about songs or singing. He was talking about life and living. True worship is life dedicated to the One you sell out for. Its life poured out in agreement with God's purposes. Once at a friend's house I saw a photograph of some graffiti on a bridge in the United Kingdom. The graffiti said, "Find something you love, and let it kill you." That's worship.

As worshippers, we're on a journey with the Creator of the universe. Our journey mandates a relationship with the One we worship, so that worship is our life. Worship is not three "up" songs followed by two "down" songs taking a grand total of 22 minutes and ending on cue because the announcements need to be next. Songs and singing are a byproduct of life lived from passion that goes all in. Our lives poured out as worship carry the viral and organic message of hope in a King.

Our adventure would be shallow confined to the walls of a church building. Our worship would be sterile limited to the pages of a hymnal. Worshipping in spirit and truth takes place "out there." *"The kind of worshippers the Father seeks"* carry His Spirit with them as they encounter heaven on earth in their daily walk.

True worship is taking the Kingdom to places that need the message of hope. It's walking in understanding as priests and kings in places where we're trained as doctors, mechanics, musicians, lawyers, teachers and endless other vocations that grant us access. Our access isn't to make enough money to live in nice houses or take our families on vacation or even to fund missions and ministries, as vital and worthy as many of those may be. We have access so we can walk deeply in spirit and truth with others, taking the glory of the King where it's needed most.

The grace to understand things is the power to effect things. Where we walk as Kingdom ambassadors, we carry the insight of the Counselor, from which we can agree with Him into the invitation of the grace of Jesus. Understanding is three dimensional and full of life.

Understanding is equipping to multiply the Kingdom of God.

Nuggets from this Chapter

- Grace gives us revelation as depth to our knowledge and the ability to apply revelation to our circumstances as wisdom.
- The Lord seeks worshippers that worship in Spirit and Truth.
- Spirit without truth invites error and Truth without breath is rigid and lifeless.
- We have access to intimacy with our Father through worshiping in Spirit and Truth.
- Knowledge, wisdom and revelation are the result of spending time with our Father and are the components to our understanding things.

Chapter 8
DOING GREAT AND GLORIOUS THINGS

In my mid-30s, I was working in corporate America and becoming increasingly dissatisfied. Some of the dissatisfaction was from corporate politics and compromise; some was simply revelation of the way I'm "hardwired." In the midst of my dissatisfaction, I read *Half Time: Moving from Success to Significance,* by Bob Buford. That book, along with some other things that happened about that time, changed everything for me.

It changed the lens through which I viewed opportunity and purpose and was the mechanism that most singlehandedly gave permission to my "want to." Most significantly, it gave me permission to explore endeavors that were more about making a difference than about personal achievement. It was an invitation into life's adventure. I accepted.

The desire to achieve great and glorious things is part of our royal DNA. It draws us beyond our natural limitations to be part of something larger than life. It's the call of Jesus into the Kingdom of God on earth as it is in heaven. It's agreeing with Him in the advancement of His purposes and plans in our lives and the lives of others.

As partakers of the benefits of grace, we're invited into this epic journey. It costs everything and is much more difficult than paths of the status quo. The shaping of credentials for involvement in the Kingdom comes at the expense of our soul, which we crucify to allow His Spirit to live in places previously reserved for us. Transformation comes from the inside out as we increasingly learn to let go of everything we otherwise squeeze for comfort and security. He has to be our only Source.

Jesus transforms you and includes you. You go places and do things you never dreamed of when you jump off the cliff of the predictable and into the unknown of a journey with Holy Spirit. I haven't arrived and I don't have it all figured out. At the same time, I've seen enough and know from experience that He is faithful.

Catching a glimpse of the vision for our destiny tempts us to believe the distance between where we are and where we're going somehow has been eliminated. Thoroughbred racehorses may see the finish line as they round the final curve, but it's up to the jockey to pace the horse until he knows it can run uninhibited for the final distance. The revelation of our God-breathed gifts and abilities tempts us to forget there's a process necessary to position us to handle the manifestation of those gifts and abilities. Just because you see it, doesn't mean you're ready for it.

Changes are necessary to realize the "what's next" in life. Dissatisfaction with compromise comes at the cost of abandon. Put another way, the only way you take hold of the future is to let go of the present. That idea as a concept is easy; the practical realities of leaving the familiar are challenging. It hurts to let go, and setting out on a quest into uncharted territory is scary.

An Invitation into Greatness

We're all invited on the journey, no matter where we are in the process. The steps along the way depend on our "Yes" and saying "Yes" depends on saying "No" to something else. The sacrifice for the adventure is giving up the mundane. Mundane is safe, safe is predictable and predictable is comforting. Drawing comfort from the control of our circumstances, we likely won't go with the Comforter to places that take us out of our self-manufactured comfort zone.

To get there we leave here. Going from glory to glory by definition requires relinquishment of the first glory to reach the second. Our destiny is the piecing together of the glories as God reveals. Each requires we step forward from the previous. Glory comes at the cost of comfort and former glories turn into present comforts. Present comforts restrict our appetites for new glories.

Most of us dream of doing big things, things that exceed the boundaries of our seemingly restraining circumstances. If we don't steward that inclination and those dreams well, they can be stolen from us, killed within us or eroded by the disappointments of life. After all, we have an enemy whose stated purpose is to steal, kill and destroy our destiny (John 10:10). Without the benefit of grace to do glorious things, it's easy to start believing our dreams are illegitimate and childish fantasy. If we fail to believe it, we fail to achieve it.

Our natural tendency to aspire beyond our apparent limitations is legitimate. We're designed for greatness; it's in the original blueprint. Humanity's fall in the Garden of Eden resulted in the limitation of our soul that causes the frustration that persists between our present reality and our God-given dreams. The existence of the frustration ever-present within us confirms that great and glorious things are, in fact, achievable through Jesus.

Kingdom life calls us to persist in our quest for the treasure of an abundant life, to not settle for "good enough." Jesus' death, burial and resurrection didn't buy us life that's "good enough." He declared repeatedly that His purpose was to give us life that's more than enough.

> *"If you have raced with men on foot and they have worn you out, how can you compete with horses?"* (Jeremiah 12:5).

We are designed to run with the horses. We are Thoroughbreds awaiting release to race toward our destiny, but our champion's heart has to learn to submit to the guidance of the One holding the reins. There is greatness within us and we know it. All too often, we'll compromise that "knowing" for the security of our bank accounts and then wonder why the Christian life seems boring. There is nothing boring about our design. Boredom and world-weariness are the result of failure to acknowledge and redeem that design from our limitations.

Just as the Thoroughbred knows instinctively it can run fast, we have an inherent passion for speed. First, however, there are trials to push through, depravity to conquer and understanding to gain between here and where God is calling us. He designed us with both the passion and the ability to win. That design is real and divinely engineered, so setbacks and failures cannot and do not invalidate our purpose.

The Risk of Passion

Just as you were, I was born with the passion and ability to win in life; nevertheless, as a criminal defense attorney I soon realized most of my efforts in that arena would be spent losing. Criminal defendants usually end up making a deal because most of them did it. They did something wrong, they know it and the prosecution can prove it, almost all of the time. Still, the defense attorney's task is providing zealous advocacy to ensure adherence to due process. Without a zealous defense bar, there is no freedom for anyone as the presumption shifts from innocence to guilt.

A career in which the vast majority of your cases are going to produce what is technically a "loss" can be frustrating without perspective. Despite the result, the legal system, your client, the Constitution and your own integrity demand you go to the courthouse and ensure the best possible outcome. At the same time, you can't own the results. You go to work, but don't squeeze the need to control the outcome.

> *"How abundant are the good things that you have stored up for those who fear you, that you bestow in the sight of all, on those who take refuge in you. In the shelter of your presence you hide them from all human intrigues; you keep them safe in your dwelling from accusing tongues"* (Psalm 31:19–20).

God provides for and protects those the watching world knows are His. Access to His *"stored up"* goodness is ours when we trust His provision. He prevails on our behalf as our zealous advocate when we rely on His protection. Living in a fallen world, there will be conspiracies against us, even lies told about us. The fork in the road is whether we rest in God's protection or attempt to protect ourselves.

When my children were young, I made them hold my hand as we walked through parking lots. We would talk along the way, and I would tell them where we were going. I didn't tell them so they could let go of my hand and run ahead. That would be dangerous. I told them so we could walk together toward the destination because I enjoyed them and wanted relationship to raise them into maturity. I don't hold their hands in the parking lot as I used to, but I still don't want them to run ahead. The enjoyment in walking toward the destination is in the companionship.

God created each of us for great and glorious things. Those things are for His glory and the advancement and fulfillment of His purposes. Our part is to agree with Him in His purposes and be conduits of His glory. As such, God does not use us; God includes us. We don't do things for God; we do things with God. Those are big differences.

Once we gain vision and purpose, the biggest challenge for many is the pace with which we approach that vision. Deciding we will be "used" by God to work "for" Him, we likely will run ahead and be about *our* purpose rather than His purpose for us. There's more than a little irony in this arrangement. When we embrace purpose so tightly that we think it's ours, we are actually choosing to exclude the One that created us for that purpose.

> *"When you have eaten your fill in this land, be careful not to forget the Lord, who rescued you from slavery in the land of Egypt"* (Deuteronomy 6:11–12).

God warned the Israelites—and you and me—what happens when we look around and think we've actually done something. If we run ahead to do things for God instead of walking with Him, we will almost certainly get to the place of some accomplishment and think we did it. In truth, we may have not depended on Him at all. Any accomplishment limited to us is always less than what He wants to accomplish with us. He'll show us where we are going, but not so we can run ahead. He wants us to enjoy the walk.

Once we taste and know the greatness of the glorious, we'll never again be satisfied with the mediocrity of the mundane. By His grace, and in our obedience to His invitation(s), He walks with us toward the fulfillment of our grand design.

We pursue a purpose that requires our effort in agreement with the One whose purpose it is. Just like the defense attorney, we are called to be zealous about the tasks of our day; we are not, however, called to own the outcome. When the world sees us owning the outcome, the only God they see in our lives is ourselves.

The whisper of God to our spirit to race toward a destiny of significance is not a prompt toward behavior. It's a reminder from our Father that by His grace we have access. We have a race to run, but we don't have a result to control. We run with disciplined passion and commitment, and then trust the results to the promises.

The race isn't easy, but the outcome is certain. Grace assures our victory when we submit to His guidance. When the time is right, He releases us to run with abandon.

Nuggets from this Chapter

- Our desire to do great and glorious things is agreeing with God in the advancement of Kingdom purposes.
- Grace invites us into an epic life of radical trust in and submission to the Father's will.
- Our design to run with the horses is harnessed for direction, not squelched for conformity.
- Culture and society invite us to compromise our great and glorious destiny for various forms of the American Dream.
- What we can achieve on our own cannot compare to the significance we are destined to achieve through Christ.

- Stepping into great and glorious requires leaving easy and predictable.

Chapter 9

ABUNDANT AND FREE

Even in the midst of life's most exciting journey, it's possible to become stuck, to feel you are running in place, or worse, bogged down and being sucked under. Being stuck is usually the result of focusing on barriers to where we know we are supposed to go. This misplaced focus results in an internal struggle that becomes funk-producing if not flat-out depressing. During one of my "stuck" times, my wife texted this verse to me:

> *"'What do you want me to do for you?' Jesus asked him.*
> *The blind man said, 'Rabbi, I want to see.'*
> *'Go,' said Jesus, 'your faith has healed you.'*
> *Immediately he received his sight and followed Jesus along the road"* (Mark 10:51–52).

My wife challenged me with this verse, and then, because she knows me well, added, "Jesus asked the blind man what he wanted. Have you told Jesus what you want or are you just stuck in feeling bad about what you have? Do you even know what you want?"

Jesus invites us to consider what we want and then ask Him for it. Without us considering what we want and asking, we likely won't credit Him with answers to our prayers. We need to know what we want and not be afraid to ask. This knowing takes our eyes off the barriers and turns our attention to Him. Our experience with Him leading up to the answers to prayer grow our faith and we follow Him.

> *"You desire but do not have, so you kill. You covet but you cannot get what you want, so you quarrel and fight. You do not have because you do not ask God. When you ask, you do not receive, because you ask with wrong motives, that you may spend what you get on your pleasures"* (James 4:2–3).

When our passions align with His purposes and advance our journey with Him, we go boldly to the throne to present the desires of our heart. We approach Him focused on His goodness and faithfulness, fixed on the destination with Him and not the barriers to our comfort. Our faith grows stronger even in the asking and our attitude changes by the hope of His promise.

Exchanging Our Limitations

Fullness in place of lack is available in Jesus. Adam's fall from ruling and reigning in the Garden resulted in the infirmities we face. Jesus restored all that was lost.

> *"For if, by the trespass of the one man, death reigned*

through that one man, how much more will those who receive God's abundant provision of grace and of the gift of righteousness reign in life through the one man, Jesus Christ!" (Romans 5:17).

The restoration of all Adam lost is available through Jesus if we'll receive His abundant provision of grace. Note what Romans 5:17 doesn't say. It doesn't say restoration comes because our parents were Christians and we grew up in a Christian home. It doesn't even say if we are born again believers we will enjoy the restoration of all that was lost in the fall.

It says *"those who receive."* More specifically, *"How much more will those who receive God's abundant provision of grace and the gift of righteousness reign in life."* In order to reign in life in a way that's consistent with the original design and purpose of Adam, we must receive God's abundant provision of grace.

That word translated "receive" in this verse is the same word translated "took" in Matthew 8:17 where Jesus *"took up our infirmities and bore our diseases."* Receiving *"God's abundant provision of grace"* is not passively sitting back and hoping something falls in our laps. It's reaching out and assertively taking it.

It's grabbing it with both hands in the same way Jesus reaches into our lives and takes the limitations of our soul in exchange for the benefits of His grace. It's His active exchange of redemption and our assertive claiming of grace by appropriating the abundance where there were limitations.

The End of Violence

I once led a meeting of about 100 or so men. At the end of that meeting, I charged them with something like "The Kingdom suffers violence and violent men take it by force" working spontaneously from my best recollection of Scripture. I said it as encouragement, to ignite them to make a difference in the world around them. My motives were right but I believe I was wrong.

In the days following that meeting, my use of that Scripture gnawed at me. Having had enough of the agitation, I decided to look at it again. Matthew 11:12 actually says, *"From the days of John the Baptist until now the kingdom of heaven has suffered violence, and the violent take it by force"* (ESV).

I had another moment of revelation as words I thought I understood took on brand-new meaning. *"From the days of John the Baptist until now"* is Jesus saying that from the time of John the Baptist until that point when He is talking, the kingdom of heaven suffered violence. The phrase *"until now"* indicates a stopping point. The violence suffered by the Kingdom stopped more than two thousand years ago.

John the Baptist was the last of the prophets and he pointed people to the fulfillment of the law. The law was satisfied with Jesus; the new covenant is grace. We keep the law from the inside out now. It's a reflection of a changed identity, not a religious effort. From the law of Moses to the time of grace, Jesus is saying there was violence in the appropriation of justification, but since Jesus, there is no more violent taking. Now there's only receiving by grace.

Without justice, mercy has no value. The blood of animals was the mechanism of justice, because the law required sacrifice for the satisfaction of justice. The violent, sacrificial repentance required by the law was completely satisfied in the violent, sacrificial death of Jesus. He fulfilled the requirement of justice. All that is left is mercy.

Mercy and grace are ours without striving, working, doing, performing or figuring out a secret code. We receive by the grace of Jesus without adding to or subtracting from what He has done. By grace we receive grace.

Courage for Grace

A gift is an offering; we don't have to receive it. We can reject the offer and do without whatever benefit it may have provided. Once accepted, however, gifts bring with them the burden of ownership. If someone gave you a house, you'd be responsible for upkeep. If someone gave you a car, you'd have to obey traffic laws and safety precautions. The receipt of the gift brings about the responsibility of ownership.

Grace comes with an invitation. The invitation of grace is not only more grace, but greater glory. If we receive what God offers us through the grace of Jesus, we can increasingly step into greater maturity. Greater maturity requires stewardship of what we already have. That stewardship includes the idea of building the Kingdom of God, not just sitting back and receiving the benefits of grace.

Jesus invites us to build His Kingdom. As exciting as Kingdom building sounds, the invitation comes with a guarantee of discomforts and challenges. Kingdom building never includes things done for our glory; rather we are invited to agree with what He is doing for His glory. By definition then, the invitation is to do things beyond our limitations and control.

Stepping out of our comfort zone to accept invitations into Kingdom building that exceed our capacity means depending on an invisible God. We have to trust in faith and stretch our comfort beyond our fears and doubts. We have to expose ourselves to embarrassment and failure, dependent on God coming through for us as the One extending the invitation. That takes courage.

Within our "Yes" to these invitations are opportunities for success as well as failure. Both success and failure accomplish the intended Kingdom purposes. What the world may deem "failures" work out the "us" that is within us to give way to God in us. Failures allow us to die to ourselves so we are equipped with humility to steward future successes. To the degree that we have adequately crucified our selfishness, we are prepared to walk into the successes.

Kingdom living guarantees there will always be more ways in which we can develop and mature. We never "arrive;" we're never "done." That's one reason living for a King and His Kingdom appeals to the deepest parts of our soul. The greatness within us hungers for the "more" He offers. To the degree we'll allow for the discomfort that comes with the stretching, we'll be increasingly equipped to receive. Our capacity to receive His "more" is directly proportional to how willing we are to give God glory where we might otherwise be tempted to think we've done something.

Shifting the Focus

We're going to mess up, but that's not the focus from heaven. The focus from heaven shifted after the sacrifice of Jesus. Instead of comparing our conduct to the law and demanding retribution for the inadequacy of our lives, we receive *the "abundant provision of grace"* of Romans 5:17.

That word *"abundant"* exceeds a fixed measure. As much as we try to quantify and define the benefit of the sacrifice, the grace we are afforded is greater. Think you are "too" bad; grace is greater. Think you are worse than everybody else; grace is plenty.

When Paul taught early believers the truth of Romans 5:17 he was confronted with the fearful argument that more grace would lead to more sin (Romans 6:1).[22] Today, many still offer that argument, insisting that teaching unbridled grace and forgiveness will somehow lead to "bad living." Nothing could be more wrong.

> *"Or do you show contempt for the riches of his kindness, forbearance and patience, not realizing that God's kindness is intended to lead you to repentance?"* (Romans 2:4).

God's kindness leads to repentance, not His judgment. Our response to the abundance of His grace is freedom. People clamber after what benefits them as a racehorse clambers after sugar cubes. We don't want less of the sweetness of freedom; we want more. We don't want less of the benefits of grace; we want more so we want more of the Benefactor.

The realization of freedom doesn't make us run to more of our own depravity. It makes us run to the Freedom-Giver. The result is we become more and more like the One we're chasing.

God's kindness and grace provide the blaring contrast against the choices of our depravity. From those dark places we wander into, His unconditional love calls us to change our mind and agree with Him. His grace informs us that His ways are better than the rebellious ways we sometimes entertain.

Abundance exceeds the boundaries of our lens and limits and is already bought and paid for. We can't get ahead of it. It's not about what we have messed up; it's about what we have available. The benefit of God's abundant grace is freedom to run in the Light without fear of our darkness blocking the view of the finish line.

Nuggets from this Chapter

- Grace is ours by grace.
- Through Jesus, we receive limitless grace and the gift of righteousness.
- Jesus died not only so we can go to heaven. He died so heaven can come to earth through us.

- Grace for the here and now is available without limit or measure.
- God's kindness, not His judgment, leads to repentance.
- Righteousness as a gift is righteousness as an identity.
- Receiving everything Jesus appropriated for us means reaching out and assertively taking it.

Chapter 10
THE LENS OF GRACE

I was raised by an Army officer and eventually became an Army officer myself. There are many good things about growing up or training in that environment. At the same time, there is a lens through which those so trained see people that can make life difficult. When the mission is critical, judgment of others can be, as well. There can be harsh, rigid assessment of people based on their performance and contribution to the mission.

After my time as an Army officer, I eventually went to law school, passed the bar, took the oath and for a season made a living standing in courtrooms arguing cases. As an advocate, I continually viewed people and their stories through my law knowledge filter. I applied that filter to things that led to the disposition of the question in the case as well as procedures compared to the rules of admission. If the opposing party tried to get inadmissible evidence into the record or question a witness in a way not allowed, I would object. It was part of my duty to my client.

Even though I no longer argue cases in a courtroom, I find myself sometimes thinking like an attorney. I don't think the word "objection," but often form a thought regarding something or someone I find "objectionable."

In doing so, I make a case against another person in my mind. This is particularly true when I perceive the other person has a responsibility to behave a certain way.

Measure for Measure

The judgment I pronounce is a revelation of the lens through which I see people. I've discovered I turn that same lens on myself. I struggle to be satisfied with anything less than excellence, so I struggle to be satisfied. I compare my behaviors, performance, accomplishments and the evidence of my success to an external standard and make a case against myself.

> *"You, therefore, have no excuse, you who pass judgment on someone else, for at whatever point you judge another, you are condemning yourself, because you who pass judgment do the same things"* (Romans 12:2).

The judgment I form against others is the standard for the judgment I form against myself. Where I compare them to expectations, I hold myself to those same expectations. Where I give grace, I am able to receive grace. I see people through a lens, and like it or not, that lens is the same for me.

> *"For the law was given through Moses; grace and truth came through Jesus Christ"* (John 1:17)

Because of Jesus, we have a choice: We can labor under the yoke of the law or we can submit to the reins of the truth. Jesus replaced the law with the truth, because the law is a subsection of the truth. The truth is the broader reality. We no longer need the law because Jesus is the whole truth and nothing but the truth.

Grace is the lens through which we are invited to view the truth. We either see through Moses or through Jesus; therefore, we see ourselves either as guilty or forgiven and will see others as we see ourselves. If you want to know what you think of yourself, consider how you think of others.

Relating with Grace

Seeing through the lens of grace became imperative when my daughter began moving into her teen years. My daughter is bright and beautiful and walks with noticeable confidence. When the bleep of teenage boys started showing up on the radar, boundaries had to be established. Even social media began demanding my attention.

The bleeping, boundaries and attention created some tension. That tension, as well as the natural discomfort we both experienced as she grew out of childhood, framed a time of needing to work some things out. It wasn't always easy or completely peaceful, as both of us had strong opinions regarding these things.

Through these years, my daughter is growing and changing as she figures out how to be the person God created her to be. In the middle of her journey, I've noticed changes in myself as well. When she was born, I was afraid. I was insecure about my ability to raise a daughter. I never felt particularly skilled at relating to women (what man does?) and suddenly I had a daughter. As far as I know, I don't have a feminine side to tap into for this particular adventure. My insecurity led me to defer to my wife for most of our daughter's needs.

I quickly realized that during this teenage transition, my engagement was mandatory. There are things about boys and boundaries that need the authority of the dad. However, I learned just as quickly that my involvement couldn't be that of a tank commander. It had to be that of an advocate. I had to be for her, and at the same time, deliver my advocacy in a way that protected her from at least some of the possible consequences of her still-developing maturity

I can't relate to her and this very important phase of life simply as an authority. I have to relate to her with grace, and I need grace as well. She needs room to figure things out, and I need opportunities to get beyond my insecurity.

We don't have it all figured out but the engagement has given me a greater appreciation for her. It's also given me a much greater appreciation for the benefit of being able to see through the lens of grace. Without that vision, this time of transition could have resulted in conflict with the potential for permanent damage to the relationship.

Not the Judge

The first time a man sat in my office and told me he was charged with a sexual crime involving a minor, I was challenged internally. I had handled many criminal cases, but they were largely misdemeanors with potential jail time and no real victim. Until that point, it was mostly people just messing up their own lives. This was different. If true, the allegations dramatically affected someone else's life.

I listened as this man, who had never been in trouble before, cried and told me of the situation. I wasn't sure what to think of the egregious nature of the allegations and was careful not to react. Finally, after quite a bit of him talking and me being quiet, I said, "I'm not sure what we'll do about your case, but what I'll offer you at this point is I won't judge you. For now, that's all I have."

I guess it sounds simple, but it was a watershed moment for me as I began to see grace, judgment, accusation and guilt differently. I started to understand with a new clarity the value of true acceptance despite the evidence of guilt. I started to comprehend, as never before, that I'm neither equipped nor asked to be the judge. There will be a judge; it's just not me. By grace, I was able to begin to see people differently—beyond the flaws and choices—and into the intent and design of their creation.

As my lens has changed for how I view others, my lens has changed for how I view myself. Not being critical of me increases my opportunities for joy. Allowing for my imperfections allows for my realization of peace. Seeing others with grace as my lens for the truth has afforded me the benefits of grace as my lens for the truth.

As He Sees Us

Grace is abundant and continues to flow for us quicker than we need it. God has an endless supply of grace and we have infinite access. Righteousness, by contrast, is given only once. That's all it takes. Our righteousness is the righteousness Jesus appropriated for us, so once stamped righteous we are righteous forever.

As children of God, we have a place of right standing with the Father because of what Jesus did. Once received, we can never give back what He did. Our spirit is righteous eternally even as our soul is being redeemed.

Righteousness has to take its place as a permanent reality in our vision of us. We have to receive the truth of the sufficiency of His sacrifice to have any hope of stepping off the life-sucking treadmill of performance and onto the road of life's greatest grace-fueled adventure. Our identity dictates that we are in right standing with God. The reality is we are His kids, but only by His grace can we see ourselves as He sees us.

Nuggets from this Chapter

- The lens of grace changes the way we see others and the way we see ourselves.
- Judgments we make against ourselves become judgments we form against others—and vice versa.
- Joy and peace result from giving and receiving grace.
- Relating to others with grace allows us to experience the joy of deep and developing relationships.
- Only by grace can we see ourselves as children of the King and walk in that identity.

Chapter 11
LOVE YOU SOME YOU

Love is discovered in the most unexpected places. For me, it was on a marriage retreat. I can tell that's going to take some explaining, after all why would discovering love be unexpected while away with my wife? Because the love I discovered on retreat wasn't for my wife. Now I really have some explaining to do. I knew I loved my wife. The surprising love I discovered while on this marriage retreat was for *me*.

It was the next to last day of the weeklong retreat and as I'm prone to do, I rose early, poured a cup of coffee and was enjoying some quiet reading. The night before, the founder and facilitator of the retreat asked if it had been a good week. "It's been great," I told him. "Great teaching and time with God, as well as between my Julie and me; great opportunities for us to set some things in order. It's been great."

It was about to go from great to transformational.

While I didn't hate me, up until that point in my life I never really loved me, either. There's a difference between self-hatred and a lack of self-love. We can not love ourselves, even not like ourselves, and still not hate ourselves. As I read in solitude that morning, Matthew 22:39 jumped off the page and into my heart as never before: *"Love your neighbor as yourself."*

To understand the full impact of these five words we need to understand the context. In Matthew 22:34–36, the Pharisees test Jesus by asking Him which commandment is the greatest. Jesus' reply to this final in a litany of questions confounds and silences the Pharisees.

> *"Jesus replied: 'Love the Lord your God with all your heart and with all your soul and with all your mind.' This is the first and greatest commandment. And the second is like it: 'Love your neighbor as yourself.' All the Law and the Prophets hang on these two commandments'"* (Matthew 22:37–40).

The greatest commandment isn't just to love God but also to love others, but that edict to love others comes with a qualifier, *"as yourself."* The limitation on our ability to keep God's greatest command to love is how much we love ourselves. *"Love your neighbor as yourself,"* means the most I can love anyone is the degree to which I love myself. Sitting on that couch drinking coffee that morning I realized I did not love myself. Never had.

This was huge. I can't love others if I don't love me. As I pondered this truth, it got personal. This was more than not being able to love the folks next door or the stranger at the grocery store. It was deeper and more compelling than that. Not loving me meant I couldn't love my wife. Not loving me meant I couldn't love God.

I was wrecked and started to cry. Once I started, I couldn't stop; I wanted to love me and I wanted to love others. I wanted to love my wife and I wanted to love God. I cried, "Please, God, help me to love me." He answered.

The Source of Everything

God began to minister to me at that point of revelation, even as I wept. First, He began to align my heart in accord with His. He showed me the constant love He has for me so I could agree with Him. I understood, for the first time, that I didn't have to generate love for Him, my wife, myself or the stranger at the grocery story. He invited me to receive love because He is the Source of love. Once I received it, I could give it away.

He was and is, in fact, the Source of everything. He was and is the Source of grace. He was and is the Source of joy, peace, patience, kindness, goodness, gentleness and self-control (Galatians 5:22–23).[23] The law can't remove or withhold from us these things that He *is* because He gives Himself to us.

Seeing God as the Source of everything removes all striving. There is no work to perform for Him to accept me. I simply receive what He offers and give it away. I receive His grace and give it away. I receive His love and give it away.

We aren't intended to be grace manufacturers; we are intended to be grace distributors. We aren't intended to be love manufacturers; we are intended to be love distributors. He flows through us and as He does, His love, grace, kindness, patience—all of His goodness fills us up, runs over the brim, and pools in puddles all around us. Everyone with whom we come in contact ends up splashed by or splashing around in His goodness. That's the way it's supposed to be.

A little while later, I was coming down the stairs by myself, praying silently. "I love you, God," I said. "I love you, too, Scott," He responded.

For the first time ever in response to what I'd received that morning on the couch I prayed, "I love me, too, God." With all that is in me, I believe He replied, "Good, then, we agree."

It's not arrogant to love yourself in agreement with the One that created you. It's arrogant not to. Pride isn't born out of knowing you are loved and agreeing; pride is fostered in the insecurity of not realizing that love and wondering if you are loved or not. Pride doesn't gloat in the deep security realized in unwavering affirmation; pride thrives in the insecurity of one constantly seeking affirmation.

The Cycle Never Ends

Since that day, God has not stopped maturing my love for Him and others by inviting me first to love me. Loving me, I am in agreement with Him and secure in His love for me. I have confidence born from the humility of receiving what I could never earn. His love is the stabilizing, empowering force that quickens and releases my love.

The only way I access His love is by the grace of Jesus. If I don't receive grace, I won't receive love. Unless I know I'm accepted because of the perfection of Jesus, I'm trapped trying to be perfect. Striving to perform, I have no grace, therefore no love, to give because I haven't received any.

It's a constant current of receiving and giving, giving and receiving. Learning how to live in grace refines our realization of grace. Until you first receive grace to some measure and then embrace it, you have no grace to give.

It's the realization and offering of love. The grace of Jesus leads to the love of the Father and the grace and love of God flow through us to others for their benefit as well as ours as we are distributors. As He flows through, we realize depths of grace and love that were only theory prior to the experience.

The Gift of Holiness

Loving ourselves doesn't come naturally and living under the Old Covenant makes it downright impossible as we are constantly reminded of our failings. By grace, we enjoy right standing with God through the righteousness of Christ, which becomes our righteousness. In Christ, we are holy because He is holy.

If we have any self-awareness whatsoever, that's likely not an idea that resonates with every area of our lives. Those things that would seem to disqualify us as holy argue with the truth of our holiness, but if we can work past the typical head-talk of self-disqualification, we are afforded an opportunity to step into the incredible gift of holiness.

No matter what we've done, there's an abundance of grace. His grace is more than enough to make us righteous no matter how much sin we've engaged in. It's a done deal, a gift. It's perfect and complete because Jesus is perfect and complete and He gives Himself to us. Jesus said, "It is finished."

Ephesians 1:4 says we *"should be holy and without blame."* If we aren't careful, we'll interpret *"should be"* as an expectation of performance. The net result of that misinterpretation is we leave the promise of His holiness behind as we try to be "good people." Good isn't holy, it's religious. Holy is holy based on the goodness of Jesus, not the goodness of us.

Next, we'll either quit or try. If we think we're too messed up, we'll give up. If we don't realize how messed up we are, we'll try harder. Neither way works. He *is*, so we can *be,* too, through Him. It's His holiness and He offers it to us as ours, for keeps.

Holiness despite our flaws offends our sense of justice and the world's system of reward for performance. Holiness as our identity depends not only on His holiness, but also on His grace. Holiness is ours to receive and root our identity in through Jesus and our receipt is available only by His immeasurable, irrevocable grace.

When we realize we are holy, we can see ourselves as He sees us despite our flaws. We can be confident and secure in our identity as righteous (Romans 5:17) and holy (Hebrews 10:10).[24] Then we can love ourselves as He loves us and stop disqualifying ourselves based on how we see us.

Nuggets from this Chapter

- We love God and others only as much as we agree with His love for us, and in response, love ourselves.
- It isn't arrogant to love yourself; it's agreement with God.
- Failure to love you fosters insecurity that produces pride.
- With God as our Source, we can love ourselves and allow His love and grace to flow through us to others.
- Holiness is part of our identity in Christ, not a measure of our performance against the law.
- The grace of Jesus allows us to receive the holiness of Jesus.

Chapter 12

THE PAIN OF APPROPRIATION

One day as I was checking the docket at the courthouse, a woman approached me and asked where a particular courtroom was. She went on to explain that she was nervous because her son was scheduled to appear on a possession of marijuana charge.

"Why does that make you nervous?" I asked.

"He could go to jail," she said.

"Did you drive here today?" I asked. After confirming that she had driven her son to the courthouse, I responded by encouraging her, saying "Well, if he goes to jail, just drive home."

"But he's my baby," she explained.

"How old is he?" I asked. After learning her son was 19, I told her bluntly but as kindly as possible, "He's not your baby. He's a grown man."

It was about that time her son joined us.

"Is this him?" I asked, and she affirmed it was.

"Listen," I said, turning my attention to him, "you are not a child anymore. Smoking weed and getting your mom to drive you to court are childish. You are a man, you are equipped to be a man and it's time to start being a man. When I was a child, I acted like one, but when I became a man, I put childish things behind me. It's time for you to do the same; you are a man and you are capable of putting childish things away."

This young man's shoulders straightened up, his eyes locked in and everything about his body language accepted the reality I was presenting him. His mom, at the same time, looked terrified. It was clear she was much less ready for him to be a man than he was.

I don't know what happened with his court case, but whatever consequences he had to deal with were a benefit to him. A misdemeanor on his record is a small price to pay if he was able to allow the consequence to draw him into responsibility.

Love allows for consequences because consequences allow for repentance. When we have to deal with the implications of our immaturity and/or depravity, we are more aware of the goodness of God. From the place of pain that results from our rebellion or immaturity, we get to choose. We can either choose to submit our lives to the goodness of God or maintain our rebellious attempts of making our own way. The choice to submit our lives back to the goodness of God is much more appealing when we have tried it without Him and are facing the reality of our choices.

We all mess up, but what we do is not who we are. Don't rescue people from their consequences and don't believe their mistakes are who they are any more than your mistakes are who you are. The kindness of the Lord leads to repentance, not the sloppy compassion or harsh judgment we may offer in its place.

It's graceful to let people realize grace by letting them deal with their own consequences. The realization of grace is born of fire, and fire burns every time. Let it happen. We aren't doing others any favors by being less than honest in our relationships. Honesty includes the willingness to allow others to choose as well as to experience the results of their choices.

If You're Feeling Salty

There was a time I was blindsided in a familiar setting. In places and in ways that I was not accustomed to being criticized, I was picked apart. It was both behind my back and to my face in front of others. It hurt and it made me angry, but I didn't respond. That hurt, too. It hurt to die to myself and to my desire to defend or even attack. I've taught on grace and written about grace and believe in grace, and now grace was being more deeply ingrained into my soul. I got a fresh glimpse of an ancient truth.

> *"Let your conversation be always full of grace, seasoned with salt, so that you may know how to answer everyone"* (Colossians 4:6).

Salt describes graceful conversation. Graceful talk is salty. Salt = grace.

Though it's most commonly used to flavor food, salt is a mineral, not an herb. Pure salt—even salt made in a lab by combining sodium and chloride—can't lose its flavor. It can be contaminated and the flavor can get lost in the contaminants, or it can be diluted and seem to lose its flavor, but salt is salty forever. Grace never changes or fades away.

In Mark 9:49–50 Jesus tells His disciples: *"Everyone will be salted with fire. Salt is good, but if it loses its saltiness, how can you make it salty again? Have salt among yourselves, and be at peace with each other."*

Grace embeds in our soul by trials (fire). In fact, grace actually *requires* our flaws be exposed and put on display. The imperfections of relationships allow the imprint of grace. Remembering that grace never loses its flavor, we recognize there is no limit to the flaws we are called to allow for in others.

Matthew 5:13[25] tells us to be the salt of the earth. It continues with the warning that salt that loses its flavor is not good for anything except trampling upon by men. The world will accept our proclamations of Jesus only as long as our flavor is His grace. Once we decide we have to defend ourselves or attack others, they have no use for our flavorless religion.

Only the pain of sin and offense flavors you with grace. In Mark 9 Jesus says *"everyone"* gets to taste the trials; we know not everyone responds with grace. Where there is the temptation, possibly even the right, to fight back, the invitation is into grace. It will hurt; dying always does. However, it will taste good to those hungering for a taste of Jesus.

Ephesians 4:29 says, *"Do not let any unwholesome talk come out of your mouths, but only what is helpful for building others up according to their needs, that it may benefit those who listen."*

The word translated "benefit"[26] here comes from original language that means, "to give grace." We can't give what we don't have, and we get grace only by experiencing problems. The problems we face afford us the opportunity to appropriate grace for the trouble.

Grace requires trouble so trouble is a perfect setup for us to receive the grace needed to understand, persevere and overcome towards our great and glorious design. From the fire, we are filled with grace as we know the goodness of our Grace-Giver. He gives us grace to be grace distributors. We get grace to give it away.

Buy the Field!

The reward is huge, but the price is unmistakable. The greatness inside screaming to get out and our undeniable desire to have an eternal impact are unlocked by selling everything else. Jesus says it like this in Matthew 13:44, *"The kingdom of heaven is like treasure hidden in a field. When a man found it he hid it again, and then in his joy he went and sold all he had and bought that field."*

Notice there was treasure discovered as well as the joy you'd expect when finding such treasure. The cost for rights to the treasure is everything we have. We can't borrow, mortgage, mitigate, negotiate or adulterate what it's going to cost. It's an all-or-nothing proposition.

Shortly after Julie and I knew we were invited into vocational ministry, I got some interesting counsel. The counsel was, "If there is anything else you can do, then do it. Only do this if you have no choice." The counsel came from a long-time pastor. He knew it costs everything.

Sometimes we give credit where credit is not due. Usually that error is born of a formula that goes something like this: bad = evil; good = holy. In other words, where we observe difficulty in our circumstances, we conclude there is an evil scheme intended for our demise, and where things are good and fun and comfortable, God is blessing us. When something isn't going the way we want, we shout at the devil and demand he stops. When things are going our way, we praise God and call Him great.

The "bad = evil; good = holy" equation doesn't add up to a sovereign God. Rather, it leaves God submitted to our circumstances. In our mind, He is great and holy as long as we are happy and comfortable. Those times we aren't feeling so loved and blessed, we turn our attention from Him to the tormentor to try to take care of the situation so God can be great for us again.

God will absolutely allow difficulty in our circumstances for our benefit even in the struggle. He is not absent in our trials. In fact, He may be most evident in our difficulties. He loves us and is not angry with us; in fact, the allowance of trouble is in accordance with His love. The destiny within us is usually born of the circumstances around us. God is faithful to show us those things He is refining if we'll look to our own refinement rather than looking for a correction to our situation.

If we'll agree with Him, He'll use our situations to grow us into greater stewards of His glory. That stewardship of Glory isn't accomplished because we are "good people." It only happens when we are refined by the fire that burns off the temporal to expose the eternal within us. Burning burns.

Julie and I can look in the eye of anyone we share our story with and tell them with sincere integrity that the cost has been enormous. And worth it. We've gone broke more than once, moved several times, been homeless by definition, stressed, doubtful, frustrated and afraid. We've been challenged, questioned, accused and rejected. We've been tempted to turn back, but once you've entered into this life that is eternal and authentic, everything else fails to satisfy. The treasure is tremendous even when the field is rocky. It's worth it; sell it all.

Nuggets from this Chapter

- Actions and choices based in our depravity allow for our realization of grace.
- Love allows consequences; consequences lead to repentance.
- Grace is impressed upon and ingrained in our soul by trials and experiences.
- The more we realize grace, the more we have to give away.

- The realization of grace comes with the realization of pain and discomfort.
- Grace requires our flaws be exposed and put on display.
- The cost of grace is high, but the treasure is eternal.

Chapter 13

THE TRANSFER OF GRACE

There was a time I was less than truthful. Nope. Let me start again. I lied. In the grand scheme of things, it was relatively harmless, but it was a lie just the same. Sin has a progressive nature so little lies make way for big lies. If we can stop the little, we'll avoid the big.

In a work situation, I had incurred an expense that I believed could be questioned based on the preferences of my boss. His bias wasn't valid or binding, nor was my decision unethical. Still, to avoid the questioning, I conveniently "lost" the receipt. It removed the red flags he would look for and avoided the scrutiny.

In this lie, my concern wasn't so much for the circumstances, as the outcome of the situation was going to be the same either way. I wasn't changing the end by my lie. I was managing perceptions of me as the results unfolded. I evaluated my behavior and knew my choice was a desire to deceive. There was no avoiding the fact: I lied.

I don't want to be a liar, and this isn't something I've struggled with. Even prior to coming to faith in Jesus, I considered myself a man of integrity. At one point, in fact, I was told I was "brutally honest." I'm not sure it was a compliment, but it was said just the same. By grace, my life now is different than before in beliefs and choices, void of so much of the depravity that once defined my lifestyle. Yet I'd allowed deceit to manifest in my behavior. I felt terrible.

Now, I know how to deal with sin. I work in ministry helping people walk free from sin and its accompanying self-condemnation every week. I knew I needed to confess, receive forgiveness and healing, repent (change my mind) and allow the grace of Jesus to cover the sin. I get it. Nevertheless, I was struggling. My imagination was running unbridled with negative thoughts regarding my future and my identity. For whatever reason, I was struggling to realize the grace of God for me in this situation.

That evening, my six-year-old son asked for a cookie. I told him that was fine and then my daughter, who is a few years older, informed me that he had already had two or three. By the time I told him to put it back, it was too late. He had eaten the cookie. "You should have told me you already had several cookies," is all I said to him.

A few minutes later, he came to me crying. I asked what was wrong and he said, "I don't want you to be mad at me." I wasn't mad and asked him why he thought I was. He replied, "Because I accidentally lied."

Now, no one accidentally lies. We choose to lie. Yet that's exactly how I felt about my choice earlier in the day. I knew it was a willful choice but felt the emotion of having made a mistake. As I listened to his six-year-old heart through tears and sniffles, I hugged him, affirmed him, forgave him and loved him. I told him he wasn't a liar.

That was it. The Lord showed me His perspective of my behavior earlier that day. He was the Father and I was the child needing assurance of His acceptance and my identity. He hugged me, affirmed me, forgave me and loved me, then told me I wasn't a liar. That's grace appropriated.

Giving it Away

When I practiced law, clients often came to my office wanting to sue someone or pursue something "on principle." Hearing those words always sounded an alarm. I would explain repeatedly to such clients that the only people who end up happy in disputes fueled by subjective principles are lawyers. Once we get months and dollars into the process, everyone except the attorneys begin to lose interest and passion for what once was an unflappable conviction.

The action of forgiveness produces an emotion more than an emotion produces forgiveness. Our emotions lie to us if we let them, and if we submit to emotions we have a hard time letting go of offenses. We end up making decisions based in hurt and from anger instead of logical steps to move forward.

Forgiveness is the release of the need for justice. It isn't releasing the truth of justice; it's simply not hanging onto control of the justice. It's allowing the consequences of a person's actions to be determined by someone or something other than the one that's hurt. For Christ followers, forgiveness is allowing God to determine justice without needing to help Him.

If you know Jesus, you know mercy. He didn't meet you with justice, but with mercy. It doesn't mean you weren't guilty; it means He isn't going to hold it against you. You are forgiven. *"Forgive us as we forgive others"* is the way He taught us to pray, but He wasn't just teaching us a prayer. He was teaching us how to live in the benefits of His grace.

Forgiveness flows through us. We aren't the source of forgiveness; we are distributors of forgiveness. Having received an abundance of forgiveness, we give it away. Giving it away positions us to receive more. We are always invited into more.

The counsel I gave clients seeking to pursue legal matters on principle didn't mean the legal system wasn't the right place to resolve disputes. It simply meant the rationale and emotions motivating litigation need to be something other than the passion of principle. Even a favorable verdict doesn't bring internal healing. Only heart level forgiveness does that.

Forgiveness is a choice. Most of us have gone through something that caused part of us to die on the inside. The pain of the experience, if allowed to fester in hurt, anger, bitterness or some other toxic emotion, can keep us from experiencing the full benefits of grace.

Transformation always goes through The Cross, and we can't believe for one second our cross is without pain. Our suffering, however, is not for the sake of suffering. It's to resurrect Him in us. We are better from things that are harder, and forgiving someone who's hurt us can be one of the hardest things we do. It's also mandatory if we are to live the epic adventure and discover the treasure God's prepared for us.

No Burden of Proof

A courtroom may be the only place in the world where taking a defensive stand means doing nothing. I have defended literally thousands of clients on various criminal matters. Prior to that, I represented thousands of insured defendants against civil claims. While the criminal standard for a conviction is more stringent than the civil standard for a finding of liability, the posture in each instance is the same: The defense carries no burden. None. Nada. Zero.

A defense attorney literally doesn't have to convince anybody of anything. The entire burden is on the prosecutor's side of the aisle. They have to gather the necessary evidence and put together a compelling argument while the defense attorney gets to sit back and poke holes in it.

The accusing party has to prove behaviors violate a law and deserve punishment. Neither the defendant nor their attorney ever has to say a word. If the plaintiff doesn't provide enough evidence to prove their case, the defense can make a single motion to the court for dismissal without ever uttering one word's worth of dispute. The entire matter can be dismissed without the defense offering one shred of evidence on their behalf.

Prior to Jesus, mankind had the burden of proof. Under the Old Covenant, we had to keep the law to attempt to stand in the presence of a holy God and try to prove we weren't guilty. Works, restraints and sacrificial offerings were the formula for a favorable verdict.

Jesus changed all that. He shifted the burden of proof from mankind, separated from God by the fall of Adam, to the accuser. Jesus was the necessary sacrifice for restoration of relationship between mankind and a holy God. His blood is the only defense we need against the accusations of our would-be prosecutor.

Jesus paid the price for the burden to shift. Because of His sacrifice of a perfect life, God no longer holds our imperfection against us. Grace replaced the previous burden.

Grace is available for everyone who chooses Jesus. Still, we continually lead out with a message of accusation when sharing the gospel. We lead out with the work of an enemy that seeks to "prosecute," separate and condemn. Jesus says to reconcile the world to Him and His grace,[27] but we take that instruction and instead all too often remind that world of their failures compared to the law.

There's no burden of proof required to receive the benefits of grace. The "burden" of Jesus is easy and light. There is no reason to exchange the easier for the greater. We can rest in Him and tell others that they can, too.

There is a time, place and need for a judge. There is also a time, place and need for a prosecutor. Those roles, however, are specialized and unique to a criminal justice system requiring them. Called to reconciliation, we don't wear those hats. They don't fit over our crown of life.

Nuggets from this Chapter

- Grace empowers us to forgive others; forgiving others is obligatory for sons and daughters of God.
- Forgiveness flows through; failure to receive it for ourselves clogs the funnel for offering it to others.
- Forgiveness isn't an emotion; it's a choice despite an emotion.
- Failure to forgive others prevents a fresh realization of freedom and makes way for bitterness to replace the joy of righteousness.
- The world needs the message of forgiveness, not condemnation.
- Forgiveness is not permission to abuse freedom, nor is it calling something that is wrong right; it's simply refusing to be the judge.
- Submitting to God as Judge releases us to our destiny.

Chapter 14
THE COMMON GROUND OF GRACE

The mission of the Church is deployment in active, assertive engagement with the world around us. Our goal is to show them the love of Jesus. The hungry need food, the thirsty need drink and those in prison are waiting for freedom. The love of the One we know as God moves us to love in a way reflective of His transformation within us. The advance is on.

It's time to let the offense loose and take the fight to the enemy. The enemy couldn't care less about our rhetoric, but quakes at the thought of our active engagement. The threat of carrying Jesus within us to those who are desperate for hope shakes the foundations of hell as the Body of Christ aligns with oneness of purpose.

Oneness of purpose is a lifestyle where others are first. It's listening to the invitations of Holy Spirit and obediently stepping in. *"For we are God's handiwork, created in Christ Jesus to do good works, which God prepared in advance for us to do"* (Ephesians 2:10).

We are transformed to be agents of transformation. We receive to give and give in such a way that glorifies God. We carry His glory to give away and put on display.

Faithful stewards of all He's given us means giving it away and multiplying it in the world around us. As we give away His gifts, we are open for more. He never fails to deliver.

Despite observations of the condition of the Church or it's ability to deliver on such a call, the Church is decidedly the delivery mechanism. There is only a "Plan A," and it is the local church. There is no "Plan B." "Church" is an intentional gathering for the purpose of celebration, connection, filling up and equipping. The application of that gathering is going out again and again to deliver the riches of a loving God to a world in dire need of Him.

We go on mission in every workplace, eating establishment, sporting event, leisure activity—in every community we operate day to day. These are our battlefields. These are where the glory of our Father shines most brilliantly stewarded by faithful receivers committed to give.

Kingdom Logistics

There's a saying in the military: "Tactics win battles. Logistics win wars." The fighting at the front lines that demand trained, skillful and courageous decisions as the bullets fly only gets you so far. Long-term success requires a supply of ammunition, fuel and food to move the force to ultimate victory. It's good to win the day, but triumph is taking back or protecting territory. That's a fair depiction of the task before us.

> *"And he gave the apostles, the prophets, the evangelists, the shepherds and teachers, to equip the saints for the work of ministry, for building up the body of Christ"* (Ephesians 4: 11–12 ESV).

The role of the "five-fold ministry" is to equip others for the work of the ministry. No matter how skillfully and thoroughly pastors or ministers equip their congregations on Sunday morning, what happens the rest of the week determines the outcome of a culture and the advancement of a Kingdom. Church leaders supply congregants with ammunition, fuel and food to move that force to broader victory well beyond the four walls of a church building.

The Kingdom doesn't advance in a building on Sunday. That's already a Kingdom stronghold, and it's the logistical supply point. The logistics of the Kingdom equip the front-line congregation with freedom, community, encouragement and knowledge for advancement into the hostile territory of our culture. Light wins the war as it travels into the dark places of the marketplace and pours mercy and grace into relationships with people who won't come to the supply point.

Taking Back Territory

In Matthew 9:27–31,[28] we read of Jesus healing two blind men. They were blind, now they can see; this is a big deal. When Jesus healed them, He *"sternly charged them"* not to tell anyone, because it wasn't time for Him to unveil His identity to the ruling authorities. Despite His warning, *"they went out and spread the news about him all over that region."*

These men didn't have a pastor instruct them to tell three of their lost friends what Jesus did and invite them to church the next week. Not only was there no expectation or requirement that they tell anyone about their miraculous new life, they were told not to talk about it. Nevertheless, just as the guilty man who tried to bear hug me in the courtroom after realizing he'd been set free, these two couldn't contain themselves.

The passion born of their encounter with Jesus exploded up and out of them without any ability for self-restraint. You can't blame them. They were blind, now they could see. They'd had no hope for a future, now their future seemed limitless. They were shackled in darkness, now they were free to run in the light. That deserved a celebration.

Sadly, too many of us on the front lines have forgotten the joy of freedom and reduced our walk with Jesus to a list of things to do—albeit with the best of intentions. We "do" all the "right" things and tell others so they can duplicate our "rightness."

Daily devotionals, church attendance, tithing and evangelism—these are good things and we should be doing them. The problem is these things often become merely part of a routine that we invite others to mimic. We aren't making disciples. We're making Sunday Morning Stepford Christians.

The men who received sight from Jesus couldn't contain themselves. Their encounter changed their lives in practically every way possible. They spread His fame from their transformation and gratitude. They were convinced everyone should know Him so they could see, too.

To reignite that conviction within yourself, remember. Remember when you were blind. Remember how it felt to be lost in the dark and then suddenly see after meeting Him. Even though it may not be as tangible as the restoration of physical sight, remember the taste of grace that released you from guilt and shame and introduced you to the Father's love. As you remember, you'll want more. As you want more, the "want" is what others will see in you. It will make Him famous. It will take back territory.

Ultimate Victory

Awhile back, we took a family trip to northern Virginia. When it was time to head back to Texas, we decided to make a quick run into Washington, D.C., as our children had shown an interest in seeing some of the monuments if the opportunity presented. We were on a tight schedule as we had a flight to catch, but didn't want to miss a chance to see at least some of our nation's capital.

We drove past the Jefferson Memorial, the Capitol and the White House, and then parked not too far from our intended destination, the Lincoln Memorial. Our path to the Lincoln Memorial took us directly past the Vietnam Veterans Memorial. We spent some time at the Lincoln and the reflecting pool, and were able to view the Washington Monument from a distance, but our time was up. We headed back to the car at a quick pace.

My father served two tours in Vietnam; he came home. I've visited the Memorial to that war on another occasion, and was impacted just as much as we raced past it this day as before. The Memorial is engraved with the names of all those who did not come home from that war. Those names are always a grim reminder of what could have been for my dad and our family. I'm always thankful.

As we moved briskly past the Vietnam Memorial for the

second time that day and I processed some emotions, Julie noticed an older Asian man along the pathway we were walking. The man was a little older than I was, but apparently has a story that causes him emotions in much the same way the realization of what could have been my story does for me. He was weeping.

Having seen him, Julie began to cry as we hurried toward our car, and about 50 yards past the man, she had to go back. She turned and jogged toward him. When she reached him, she comforted him and asked if she could hug him. (If you know her, you aren't surprised). He smiled and welcomed her comfort. That was it. We had to go. Time was up.

Holy Spirit is the Comforter and He lives within every born-again believer in Jesus. He lives in us not only because we need comfort, but also because other people do. Julie heard Holy Spirit's invitation to comfort this stranger, obediently stepped in and took back territory. I have no way of knowing who the man was, why he was weeping or whether he'd ever met Jesus before that day. I know he has now, even if he doesn't yet realize it.

Giving comfort is a testimony of Jesus, with or without words. The expression of the heart of God happens through people with people. People around us are weeping, and we get to connect heaven to earth when we notice earth and offer heaven. There is a grace common to all of us that invites us to connect. It is in the connection of people where the fellowship of Holy Spirit is most evident.

Nuggets from this Chapter

- Grace invites us into the Kingdom, not into seclusion.
- As recipients of grace, our great and glorious commission is to carry grace to a world in need of grace.
- We gather as a church to be encouraged and refreshed before going out to engage in the battle.
- Those in the most need of mercy and grace are found in the marketplace, not the mercy and grace logistical supply point.
- The role of church leadership is to equip believers to carry the Kingdom to dark places.
- Believers carry spiritual gifts, wisdom, favor and grace to the marketplace, proclaiming Jesus and claiming territory.
- The common ground of grace connects us to others in need of grace.
- Grace, itself, sparks our memory of grace to reignite our passion for grace.

Chapter 15

SPOTTING THE ISSUE

The method law schools use to teach law is simple: read. Sounds easy enough, right? It's not. The nightmarish stories you may have heard of law students reading literally all night then rushing to class to be bombarded by questions specifically designed to expose their lack of understanding are true. Because of the nature of the study of law, it's the most effective method. There are no shortcuts. You dig in and read. And read. And read.

It's not unusual for professors to assign hundreds of pages of reading each night. By the end of the semester, law students have read literally tens of thousands of pages of narratives describing how courts have settled cases. Then come the exams. You guessed it, more reading. Law school exams consist of reading long narrative descriptions of situations from which the task is to identify the potential legal issues and apply the appropriate law toward a compelling legal argument. Success in each class typically stands (or falls) on one grade per semester: the infamous Final Exam.

The Final is the framework—a/k/a your only chance—to show the professor how much you know (or don't know) about the pertinent law. Understanding the intricacies and nuances of the law are imperative, but if you haven't learned how to spot the issues from the cases you read in preparation throughout the semester, you're in trouble come exam time. Properly identifying the issue(s) is the foundation for being able to pass the exam, and therefore, the course. An entire semester's worth of work, countless sleepless nights spent reading, reading and reading, can all be for naught if you fail to identify correctly the issues in question.

The same is true in life. I see and hear people misidentify therefore mishandle the issues of life all the time. Without correctly identifying the issue and getting to its source, finding the solution to a problem in life is all but impossible. Life's problems stem from one of several sources:

- **Ourselves** – Bad choices bring consequences and require us to change our mind if we want to change the behaviors that affect our outcomes. When we break it, we buy it. If we don't own our part of a bad deal, expecting God to "zap" us into a better deal leads to frustration, discouragement and possibly even doubt.

- **Other People** – Living in community with other people (even church people) in a fallen world leads to offenses, wounds and problems. Part of the purpose of community is to learn to live with grace toward others in granting the forgiveness we've been granted.

As we grow in knowledge of our identity, we become increasingly less susceptible to offense.

- **The Devil** – This catchall source gets much more credit than he deserves. While there are legitimate spiritual attacks, many circumstances come from our choices, and many more are God calling us into something bigger by growing our character through adversity.

- **God** – Just as the devil gets more attention than he deserves, God often is the scapegoat for our choices. A skewed picture of the nature of God leads us to attribute things that aren't of Him to Him. It also removes from us the benefits of relationship, as He wants us to mature as sons and daughters. Rather than living as children of the King, we're reduced to rubbing a genie lamp while crossing our fingers that our three wishes will make life better.

If we get the issue wrong, we have little chance of applying the proper solution. Often, our first instinct is to assign blame. Believing blame is always necessary to assess the issue is a faulty premise that never leads to a graceful solution.

No Blame Required

When I was practicing criminal defense law, the constant contention of that adversarial system would wear on me. I would have to take a break and get away from time to time to clear my lens. My lens would get cloudy from a residue of accusation, explanation, lies born of self-preservation, consequences and other aspects of the system. I would get a bit jaded in my view of humanity—and I wasn't the only one. The criminal law bar generally can be cynical and sarcastic, with harsh language and vices to lube the friction.

All too often, I have chosen to play the part of judge, prosecutor or defense attorney where there is no court of law. In life's everyday interactions, there are disappointments and disagreements that draw a reaction that is born out of an illusion. The illusion is that we need a verdict regarding right or wrong in every circumstance. Where the verdict is "wrong," as it often is because of the flawed human condition, we think there needs to be an assessment of blame. There doesn't.

There is no freedom in the need for justice. Freedom is grace based. It has to be, or the busyness of blame will overcome any of the potential peace of freedom.

Freedom starts and ends with identity. When we realize who we are and why, we are at ground zero of peace. That identity is not earned and doesn't have to be defended. We don't have to prove anything because we didn't do anything in the first place. Jesus died to make us righteous by His sacrifice. Where we are willing to agree with Him, we enjoy the benefit of His victory.

When our identity is based in His perfection and sacrifice, we can stop. We can stop defending ourselves, and we can stop prosecuting others to elevate ourselves by comparison. Every mistake does not require a verdict. Every shortcoming doesn't call for an explanation. Every flaw doesn't need assignment of a cause.

Today things are going to happen. Grocery clerks, coworkers, friends, kids, spouses and myriad others are going to mess up. So are you. It's okay. Those mistakes don't demand a verdict. Rest in the peace of grace. Rest in Jesus.

A Unique Benefit

In John 9, Jesus comes across a blind man. Immediately, His disciples ask Him a question based in the faulty premise of blame: *"Rabbi, who sinned, this man or his parents, that he was born blind?"* (v. 2).

Jesus answers in verse 3, *"Neither this man nor his parents sinned," said Jesus, "but this happened so that the works of God might be displayed in him."*

Jesus rejected outright the premise of their question. They were seeing through the lens of justice, but He was here to do a lens transplant. Jesus came to put in a grace lens where the justice lens had been relied upon. As was their nature, the disciples were seeking justice. Instead, Jesus was offering glory by His grace. Grace proclaims the glory of God while justice only glorifies (or disqualifies) the ability of man. Justice examines the temporary voids we experience in a fallen world; grace invites us into the glory of eternity here and now.

Their perspective was and often ours is the default perspective. We see this in Acts 28 when Paul was bitten by a snake, and as the snake still hung from his hand, the islanders who'd initially welcomed him with *"unusual kindness"* (v. 2) accused him of being a murderer for such a thing to happen. They needed to rely on the familiarity and predictability of justice.

When Paul didn't die, they proclaimed him not a murderer but a god (v. 6). These people, who'd never heard of Jesus, needed to rely on the familiarity and predictability of justice over the sloppiness of grace. Grace, however, is uniquely available to us even prior to any realization of salvation or transformation.

Humankind isn't stuck in the ramifications of justice. We don't have to assess blame with accusations of murder or other offsets to offenses we experience. We are given the privilege of a common grace[29] from which not even the angels benefit.

"For if God did not spare angels when they sinned, but sent them to hell, putting them in chains of darkness to be held for judgment" (2 Peter 2:4).

The angels that sinned were sent straight to hell as part of their rebellion against God; none were spared. We rightly could receive the same, yet humans are afforded the common grace of opportunity for redemption. We get a shot at another shot. While not all will know Jesus as their Savior, Jesus died for all to offer all the possibility.

Every one of us can receive the benefit of Jesus and every one of us can see the evidence of God whether we know Jesus as Savior or not:

- There is the evidence of testimony in nature: *"Yet He has not left Himself without testimony: He has shown kindness by giving you rain from heaven and crops in their seasons; He provides you with plenty of food and fills your hearts with joy"* (Acts 14:17).

- There is also the common grace that shows itself in our morality. Even where mankind rejects Jesus, the evidence of God is on display in the restraints man imposes from within. We restrain from completely unleashing the hell of our fall by the grace of this morality: *"Indeed, when Gentiles, who do not have the law, do by nature things required by the law, they are a law for themselves, even though they do not have the law. They show that the requirements of the law are written on their hearts, their consciences also bearing witness, and their thoughts sometimes accusing them and at other times even defending them"* (Romans 2:14–15).

- Good and bad, right and wrong are ingrained and rewarded in society. God put a mechanism in place to restrain us (saved or lost) where we won't restrain ourselves for the benefit of everyone that might otherwise be a potential victim: *"Let everyone be subject to the governing authorities, for there is no authority except that which God has established. The authorities that exist have been established by God"* (Romans 13:1).

Common grace testifies of God through sunsets, sunrises, mountains and oceans, as well as the cry of a baby or the laugh of a child. That same common grace provides restraint to keep order and protect us from our otherwise depraved nature. Still, there is a more excellent grace available: the saving grace of Jesus. Saving grace doesn't' seek to restrain; it unleashes us to walk in purpose and passion in the context of the Kingdom.

While those of us that know Jesus as Savior have tapped into His saving grace for an eternal benefit, we must not cease to value the common grace we enjoy with the rest of humanity. Common grace gives us a place to meet the world; receiving the goodness of God's grace manifest in those that disagree with our theology. When we are zealous about saving grace without meeting people at God's common grace, we are likely seeing through the lens of justice to affirm our beliefs while leaving behind the ones those beliefs should be pointing us toward as evidence that we love others as we love ourselves.

We can meet in the beauty and humanity we all experience to forge relationships. In relationship, we put the saving grace of Jesus on display to those who might not otherwise be interested. We must first meet others just as Jesus met us, as humans, if we are ever to know them as siblings.

Nuggets from This Chapter

- If we don't properly assess why something is happening, we won't apply proper solutions.
- Blame is not required for every circumstance we experience.
- When we know who we are in Christ, we can stop being defensive to protect ourselves.
- All too often, we choose to play the part of judge or prosecutor even though there doesn't need to be a trial.
- Since we are forgiven and free, we can meet people where they are; we don't have to prove them wrong.
- Common grace allows for connection with the world

where they may disagree with us regarding saving grace.
- From relationship formed in common grace, we can share our lives of saving and transforming grace.

Chapter 16

GREATER GLORY

We are born with an inherent desire to accomplish great and glorious things, but when we step from where we are to where we think we're going, invariably we have to go back and cover some bases. "First things first" isn't a catchy phrase; it's wisdom. The first thing must be first so second and third things enjoy the benefit of the first thing being in place. If we circumvent the order, the resulting accomplishment (if any) will be vulnerable to the faults of an improper foundation.

The prompting toward a glorious destiny isn't because we're special; it's because we're invited by grace. The call into greatness is part of a larger call into a greater greatness than any individual can achieve. It's a corporate call with a Kingdom context. The corporate call requires the ability to be relational, and the Kingdom context ensures the ultimate glory isn't reserved for an individual or even the corporate actors.

One thing builds upon the next. We can't take shortcuts and believe the progress we observe is sustainable. The legitimate vision for a significant role with an eternal impact depends on the proper order of relationship. The order of relationship to build upon is this:

1. **Consecration** – Setting our life apart from the world to know Jesus intimately. This is where The Father establishes our identity in Him.

2. **Companionship** – Intimately living with others where there is authentic and transparent connection. Here is where iron sharpens iron and the transformation that began in consecration works out through our soul.

3. **Community** – Being part of the body with Christ as the Head and honoring Him and those gifted and equipped differently than we are. It's a symphony of His design played through individuals making up His orchestra.

4. **Reconciliation** – Arriving at the place of significance and impact, which is different from what we envisioned at the inception of our journey. This is accepting others and joining with them and their flaws in grace. It's bestowing honor to accomplish the advancement of the Kingdom.

By the time we reach our destiny, we realize our destiny was never about us. It's a glorious destiny, but it's His glory, not ours. Arriving at the conclusion of the grace-fueled journey, we rejoice that He receives glory. It's in rejoicing in His glory we realize the riches of the treasure we've discovered along the way.

Consecration

Success is more difficult than failure and it's easier to walk secure in our identity when challenged by circumstances than when relaxing in comfort. If you've been on this journey long, you may have experienced the irony of this truth yourself. Failure and challenging circumstances present greater opportunities to live what we believe than success and comfort.

It's natural to desire success. Everyone wants to win and enjoy the spoils of victory. Some even have created doctrines to bolster the belief that we're entitled to success as part of our faith. There may be some truth in such a doctrine, but if so, there has to be more to the story.

In 1 Kings 9, God tells King Solomon He will agree with Solomon's prayers and bless not only the temple but also the king's house and *"all that Solomon desired to build"* (v. 1 ESV). It wasn't just the "religious stuff," but the desires of Solomon's heart, as well. God said He would "consecrate," or set apart as Holy, Solomon's work forever (v. 3).

Solomon inherited an extraordinary earthly kingdom and enjoyed great favor in the advancement of that kingdom. God promised Solomon perpetual favor with one caveat: keep First things first. God's only condition was that Solomon continue to walk in the ways of the

Lord. If he would maintain *"integrity of heart and uprightness"* then his throne over Israel would last forever (vs. 4–5 ESV).

Solomon didn't consecrate the kingdom; God did. It was God's choice to set it aside for His purposes and His glory. Solomon didn't have to work to do that. His only responsibility was to maintain God as God in his heart and mind.

But Solomon turned from the Lord and chose other gods. The consequences of his choices stripped him and his heirs of much of his kingdom. The consequences weren't because he was "bad" or didn't follow the "rules." The consequences were because Holy and not Holy don't mix.

Solomon turned to other gods and the One and only God does not compete. He put an end to the not Holy not to punish Solomon but to protect what He declared as Holy.

God wants to bless us and consecrate our lives and work. Sustaining His blessings depends on understanding that He is the One doing the consecrating, not us. Agreeing with Him during times of blessing as much as during times of challenge, we can perpetually reap the benefit of His magnificent promises. However, faced with the comfort of success, our human hearts are tempted to compromise. Compromise always invites idolatry.

The idols of success creep in incrementally. The fall isn't overnight. It's in the seemingly benign choices of forgetfulness and laziness as we relegate God to second where He was first. Only by grace do we keep First things first. Learning to protect the desperation of our prayers and continuing to seek consecration from the One that makes things Holy, we can be as successful in success as He made us from our failures.

Companionship

In Philippians 2:12 Paul instructs us to *"work out our salvation."*[30] We know salvation is by grace and not any "work" we can ever accomplish. Paul's instruction isn't to earn salvation, but rather to build on the foundation of consecration that is ours at the moment of salvation when the Father sets us apart as His children.

That "working out" can't take place in the security and seclusion of consecration. It takes place in intimate relationship with others. Once we enjoy the maturity that comes with knowing who we are from the inside out, we begin to work that truth out from the core to the surface.

God speaks our identity to our spirit, which is perfect when renewed by His Spirit. However, our imperfect soul is the filter through which we hear the Father's voice. Imperfections in our soul create misinterpretations and blind spots. Companionship helps us identify the misconceptions and blind spots of our soul.

Marriage is the epitome of companionship and the prime example of how and why we need to work things out within ourselves. We can know we are sons and daughters of God all we want, but the unredeemed parts of our soul that need maturing and daily death are on full display in the close proximity of companionship. Sharing life with one another, conflict and the need to work through conflict to resolution are part of the plan.

Marriage is not nor was it ever meant to be a Hallmark® card. God's plan for marriage is to put His full nature on display, so any part of us that supersedes any part of Him in us has to go. There's no better way to get from here to there on the journey toward less of us and more of Him than the humility and selflessness necessary for intimate companionship.

Living close to another exposes every part of our soul that wants to self-protect, self-provide and self-promote. That exposure forces us to choose to either live up to the character of our identity or maintain our role as orphans. We choose to either give in to fears, doubts and lies that originate within ourselves or trust the Truth of who we are at the risk of pain or rejection.

The process of working out our salvation prepares us to continue our quest for destiny. Without the type of methodical perseverance that maintains relationship when it hurts, our character never comes in line with our identity. We end up jumping around from association to association, with the only constant being the immature orphan we foster within ourselves. Grace provides the perseverance to develop our character as well as the courage to risk rejection.

Community

When the real reason for something is different from the expectation of that thing's purpose, there's bound to be a problem. Unfulfilled expectations always lead to disappointment. In the wake of disappointment, we can either get mad or correct our perspective. The truth is, when it's all said and done, it's not the "something" that has a problem, it's us.

I realize that all sounds somewhat cryptic, but I'm speaking in broad generalities because the problem of expectations has a broad reach. Refining the subject of expectations to a more narrow focus, most of us want something out of church that it was never intended to provide.

We go to church because we want to be accepted, agreed with and affirmed. We go to church because we want life to be "good" and we tend to equate church with a "good purpose" and with "good things" in general. When something happens in or around church that disappoints our expectation of "good" (it's only a matter of time), we feel justified in judging those happenings and that church.

Most of us stand on our justification as we complain, conspire and ultimately abandon the community for failing to live up to our expectations. This is true for novice and seasoned churchgoers alike. From the back pew to the front-row leadership team, everyone is susceptible to being disappointed by church.

But what if the whole idea and purpose of church is not so we can feel good? What if the real reason for church is to live and serve in close enough proximity with other flawed people that so those flaws come out in community? Could it be the real opportunity for church emerges from the exposure of our failings and the failings in others?

In living with others, we are going to offend and be offended. The closer the proximity, the more certain and more frequent the offenses. Out of those offenses emerge opportunities to give and receive grace. We seek the same grace Jesus afforded us and give it to others. We receive grace from others as we seek grace for them and us.

The display of grace among people who need and offer grace is the display of Jesus. Jesus is not on display in our pretense of perfection, but He is available for the world to see in us through our weakness. In our weakness, He is strong. In our flaws, we rely on His grace.

Living together as the Church gives a dying world the chance to see Life as they see Jesus in us. Life doesn't show up in our make-believe perfection, but in our gracious acceptance of our imperfections and the imperfections of others. Authentic relationships reveal authentic flaws and authentic flaws require authentic grace.

Reconciliation

The bad news is we can't do it; the good news is we don't have to. We really have nothing to prove or accomplish to advance us in favor or blessings. We have no burden to protect God's reputation or advance His cause of our own initiative. What we have is the opportunity to join Him in what He's doing.

> *"As God's co-workers we urge you not to receive God's grace in vain"* (2 Corinthians 6:1).

In this passage, Paul writes about the opportunity to walk as an ambassador of Christ and offer the message of reconciliation to a world that urgently needs to be reconciled to God. The only thing that qualifies us to be ambassadors of Christ and ministers of reconciliation is that we are reconciled to Christ. He is the qualifier. He is the Savior. We just receive.

In the same way we were lost and dead in our separation from God, others still are. Jesus commissions us to bring them the good news of His salvation, but our delivering that good news doesn't make Him any less the Savior. Only Jesus has the capacity to save. We simply carry the message, then stand back and marvel as the Living Word reconciles the lost to Himself.

Agreement with Christ as King in the advancement of His Kingdom is acceptance of an invitation into life and living. Engaging with the lost and broken enlivens us as much as it transforms them, and the receive-give-repeat cycle perpetuates and multiplies. We are encouraged and alive in the purpose that comes with accepting invitations into the eternal, even as we are otherwise bound by the temporal.

Paul's words in 2 Corinthians 6:1 are clear. We are on a quest with Him, not for Him. There's a big difference between doing something "with" or "for." We do nothing "for" Christ. We take the message of reconciliation to the lost only walking "with" Him.

Doing anything "for" God is burdensome and lifeless. It's the fulfillment of an obligation that never existed toward a purpose we can never accomplish. It's hoping a distant father notices the striving child and grants approval based on performance. It's orphan behavior.

As children of God the Father through Christ the Son, we are in Him. We can't get any more "in," and we don't need to "do" anything else. He invites us to experience Him in an infinite variety of ways through our finite earthly existence. We are sons and daughters in Him with no need to prove it or earn it.

Simply Yes and Amen

> *"For no matter how many promises God has made, they are 'Yes' in Christ. And so through him the 'Amen' is spoken by us to the glory of God"* (2 Corinthians 1:20).

Jesus is our Advocate and His sacrifice says "Yes" to the fulfillment of God's promises and the redemption of the infirmities He has taken. We offer our "Amen" to receive the delivery of the promise and redemption of our infirmities.

Amen is simply a word of agreement to welcome the promises of God to our circumstances. When we say "Amen," we say, "I accept it on earth as it is in heaven." It's the same agreement Mary gave when the angel told her she would conceive immaculately and give birth to the Savior: *"'I am the Lord's servant,' Mary answered. 'May your word to me be fulfilled'"* (Luke 1:38).

Our posture for prayer changes with the realization of grace. We pray from a thankful place for the promise made through His resurrection. We approach Him thankful for the redemption of things we lack, as we know He joyfully wants to pour out His favor and redeem our limitations. We pray boldly to receive what we need to remedy our limitations for reigning in life.

In Jesus, the whole treasure is ours: love, joy, peace, patience, kindness, goodness, faithfulness, gentleness and self-control. We can reign victoriously, as originally intended for Adam. The redemption of the curse is waiting for us to lay hold of and the blessings are eternal and abundant.

It's all in His grace. The grace of Jesus holds the entirety of His promises for us. We don't have to know the secret combination to unlock a hidden treasure room. Grace reveals the treasure and throws open the door. By grace, we enter in, proclaiming, "Amen. May your word to me be fulfilled."

Nuggets from this Chapter

- Walking in order toward our destiny fosters our development into maturity.

- We first must set our lives apart as adopted children of God to know our identity for the foundation to walking toward destiny.
- Companionship requires intimacy and intimacy flushes out insecurities that need to be aligned with our identity realized when consecrated.
- Community allows for the diversity of gifts to be fitted together for multiplication of impact.
- The invitation of grace is into the love and adoption of the Father, from which we can walk in healthy relationship and community to reconcile the world to Him.
- Grace allows us to agree with the Father and receive the treasure His grace appropriates.

WORKS CITED

Wayne Grudem, "Common Grace," *Systematic Theology: An Introduction to Biblical Doctrine*. Leicester: Inter-Varsity, 2007; Michigan: Zondervan, 1994. Print.

NOTES

[1] John 8:1–11.

[2] *"He has made us competent as ministers of a new covenant—not of the letter but of the Spirit; for the letter kills, but the Spirit gives life. Now if the ministry that brought death, which was engraved in letters on stone, came with glory, so that the Israelites could not look steadily at the face of Moses because of its glory, transitory though it was, will not the ministry of the Spirit be even more glorious? If the ministry that brought condemnation was glorious, how much more glorious is the ministry that brings righteousness! For what was glorious has no glory now in comparison with the surpassing glory. And if what was transitory came with glory, how much greater is the glory of that which lasts!*

Therefore, since we have such a hope, we are very bold. We are not like Moses, who would put a veil over his face to prevent the Israelites from seeing the end of what was passing away. But their minds were made dull, for to this day the same veil remains when the old covenant is read. It has not been removed because only in Christ is it taken away. Even to this day when Moses is read, a veil covers their hearts. But whenever anyone turns to the Lord, the veil is taken away.

Now the Lord is the Spirit, and where the Spirit of the Lord is, there is freedom. And we all, who with unveiled faces contemplate the Lord's glory, are being transformed into his image with ever-increasing glory, which comes from the Lord, who is the Spirit."

[3] Romans 8:17.

[4] *"Surely he took up our pain and bore our suffering."*

[5] *Lambanó*, retrieved at http://biblehub.com/greek/2983.htm (Mar. 2017).

[6] Ibid.

[7] *Astheneia,* retrieved at http://biblehub.com/greek/769.htm (Feb. 2017).

[8] Ibid.

[9] *"Taste and see that the Lord is good; blessed is the one who takes refuge in him."*

[10] *"For if, by the trespass of the one man, death reigned through that one man, how much more will those who receive God's abundant provision of grace and of the gift of righteousness reign in life through the one man, Jesus Christ!"*

[11] Romans 6:6, 8, 11: *"We know that our old sinful selves were crucified with Christ so that sin might lose its power in our lives. We are no longer slaves to sin... And since we died with Christ, we know we will also live with him...So you also should consider yourselves to be dead to the power of sin and alive to God through Christ Jesus"*

[12] *"Come to me, all you who are weary and burdened, and I will give you rest. Take my yoke upon you and learn from me, for I am gentle and humble in heart, and you will find rest for your souls. For my yoke is easy and my burden is light."*

[13] *Osteb* from the original *astab,* and including *asabbe,* retrieved at http://biblehub.com/hebrew/haatzabbim_6091.htm (July 2017).

[14] *"Hand this man over to Satan for the destruction of the flesh, so that his spirit may be saved on the day of the Lord."*

[15] *"I have told you these things, so that in me you may have peace. In this world you will have trouble. But take heart! I have overcome the world."*

[16] *"For we do not have a high priest who is unable to empathize with our weaknesses, but we have one who*

has been tempted in every way, just as we are—yet he did not sin."

[17] *"Consider him who endured such opposition from sinners, so that you will not grow weary and lose heart. In your struggle against sin, you have not yet resisted to the point of shedding your blood."*

[18] *"For our light and momentary troubles are achieving for us an eternal glory that far outweighs them all."*

[19] *Stephanos*, retrieved at http://biblehub.com/greek/4735.htm (Mar. 2017).

[20] John 10:10: *"The thief comes only to steal and kill and destroy; I have come that they may have life, and have it to the full."*

John 3:16: *"For God so loved the world that he gave his one and only Son, that whoever believes in him shall not perish but have eternal life."*

[21] *"The twenty-four elders fall down before him who sits on the throne and worship him who lives forever and ever. They lay their crowns before the throne and say: 'You are worthy, our Lord and God, to receive glory and honor and power, for you created all things, and by your will they were created and have their being.'"*

[22] *"What shall we say, then? Shall we go on sinning so that grace may increase?"*

[23] *"But the fruit of the Spirit is love, joy, peace, forbearance, kindness, goodness, faithfulness, gentleness and self-control. Against such things there is no law."*

[24] *"And by that will, we have been made holy through the sacrifice of the body of Jesus Christ once for all."*

[25] *"You are the salt of the earth. But if the salt loses its saltiness, how can it be made salty again? It is no longer good for anything, except to be thrown out and trampled underfoot."*

[26] *Charin*, retrieved at http://biblehub.com/ephesians/4-29.htm (July 2017).

[27] Corinthians 5:18–19: *"All this is from God, who reconciled us to himself through Christ and gave us the ministry of reconciliation: that God was reconciling the world to himself in Christ, not counting people's sins against them. And he has committed to us the message of reconciliation."*

[28] *"And as Jesus passed on from there, two blind men followed him, crying aloud, 'Have mercy on us, Son of David.' When he entered the house, the blind men came*

to him; and Jesus said to them, 'Do you believe that I am able to do this?' They said to him, 'Yes, Lord.' Then he touched their eyes, saying, 'According to your faith be it done to you.' And their eyes were opened. And Jesus sternly charged them, 'See that no one knows it.' But they went away and spread his fame through all that district."

[29] Wayne Grudem, "Common Grace," *Systematic Theology: An Introduction to Biblical Doctrine*. (Leicester: Inter-Varsity, 2007; Michigan: Zondervan, 1994).

[30] *"Therefore, my dear friends, as you have always obeyed—not only in my presence, but now much more in my absence—continue to work out your salvation with fear and trembling."*

Made in the USA
Middletown, DE
04 December 2017